What readers are saying about IN 30 MINUTES® guides:

Google Drive & Docs In 30 Minutes

"I bought your Google Docs guide myself (my new company uses it) and it was really handy. I loved it."

"I have been impressed by the writing style and how easy it was to get very familiar and start leveraging Google Docs. I can't wait for more titles. Nice job!"

Genealogy Basics In 30 Minutes

"This basic genealogy book is a fast, informative read that will get you on your way if you are ready to begin your genealogy journey or are looking for tips to push past a problem area."

"The personal one-on-one feel and the obvious dedication it took to boil down a lot of research into such a small book and still make it readable are the two reasons I give this book such a high rating. Recommended."

Twitter In 30 Minutes

"A perfect introduction to Twitter. Quick and easy read with lots of photos. I finally understand the # symbol!"

"Clarified any issues and concerns I had and listed some excellent precautions."

D1571249

LinkedIn In 30 Minutes

"This book does everything it cla... ...gives you a great introduction to LinkedIn and gives you tips on how to make a good profile."

"I already had a LinkedIn account, which I use on a regular basis, but still found the book very helpful. The author gave examples and explained why it is important to detail and promote your account."

Excel Basics In 30 Minutes

"Fast and easy. The material presented is very basic but it is also accessible with step-by-step screenshots and a friendly tone more like a friend or co-worker explaining how to use Excel than a technical manual."

"An excellent little guide. For those who already know their way around Excel, it'll be a good refresher course. Definitely plan on passing it around the office."

Learn more about IN 30 MINUTES® guides at in30minutes.com

Crowdfunding
Basics
In 30 Minutes

How to use Kickstarter, Indiegogo, and other crowdfunding platforms to support your entrepreneurial and creative dreams

Michael J. Epstein

IN 30 MINUTES® Guides

Published by i30 Media Corporation
Newton, Massachusetts

CONTENTS

Contents

Just a few short years ago, if you wanted to start a business selling a new kind of bicycle or raise money to make an independent movie, you had no choice but to scrape together funding on your own or hope a generous friend or relative might be willing to put up seed capital. Now it is possible to look to the online masses and leverage crowdfunding, not only to raise money to fund your idea, but also to generate excitement and build a community of supporters. Crowdfunding is truly a game changer for those of us without easy access to capital for our projects!

Crowdfunding involves raising money through small contributions from a large number of people using online platforms. It has the potential to level the playing field for independent creators, entrepreneurs, and artists. Crowdfunding can also bring together communities, driving the pooling of resources to support people in need, to overcome bureaucratic or logistical obstacles, or to provide public benefit.

Crowdfunding is a powerful trend, and has wide-reaching implications. It has the potential to broaden grassroots support for new art, cutting-edge business concepts, and local causes, thereby weakening the hold of conservative gatekeepers who might otherwise be unwilling to risk supporting ideas that are too bold or innovative. There are now numerous crowdfunding services and accompanying support tools, making crowdfunding viable for an increasingly wide range of projects and causes, from the personal to the professional.

But crowdfunding is imperfect, and not every campaign is successful! For your campaign to reach its fundraising and project goals, a lot of hard work and careful planning will be required. You must consider the benefits and pitfalls of running a campaign and ensure that your enthusiasm is tempered with a realistic understanding of what crowdfunding can achieve. In the coming chapters, we'll take a look at whether crowdfunding is right for your project, and how you can maximize your chances for success.

The growth of crowdfunding

I became interested in crowdfunding in 2011 when I realized that it could help bring together a group of local artists to make an independent feature film. Because film is relatively unusual to the independent arts community in Boston, the idea was met with great enthusiasm. Now, five years later, I have not only used crowdfunding to grow a filmmaking career from scratch, but I have also consulted on dozens of film, theater, music, entrepreneurial, and cause-related crowdfunding projects.

In addition, I have backed more than 500 projects launched by other people on a dozen different crowdfunding platforms. Among these projects, I have seen massive successes and heartbreaking failures. These outcomes have provided important lessons in designing and executing crowdfunding campaigns, as well as working to fulfill promises to backers as projects are completed.

There has been exponential growth in crowdfunding over the past few years. Kickstarter has been leading the wave. Consider these Kickstarter statistics:

➤ More than 350,000 projects launched.

➤ More than 120,000 projects funded.

➤ Over 35 million individual pledges.

➤ Total pledges: more than $3 billion.

The population at large is now aware of crowdfunding as an alternate method for raising capital. With its widespread acceptance, crowdfunding could be the ticket to turning your great idea into a reality!

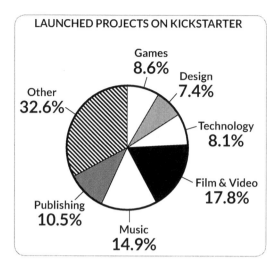

LAUNCHED PROJECTS ON KICKSTARTER

Games 8.6%
Design 7.4%
Other 32.6%
Technology 8.1%
Film & Video 17.8%
Publishing 10.5%
Music 14.9%

As familiarity and confidence spread, crowdfunding will continue on a growth trend for a long time to come. In fact, as traditional entertainment, manufacturing, retail, and publishing industries lose their monopolies on mainstream consumerism, opportunities for the crowdfunded creation of products will be ever more plentiful. It just might be the right time to look at crowdfunding for your project or cause.

Examples of great crowdfunding projects

While crowdfunding has become popular with celebrities and founders with significant fan and financial bases, the stories presented here will focus on creators with more modest resources. These examples serve as models for connecting enthusiastic niche communities with campaigns based on bold ideas or important needs. Crowdfunding is truly available to just about anyone with a great idea and a willingness to work hard to get it out there.

Consider the following examples:

➤ **Maxwell Bogue, Peter Dilworth, and Daniel Cowen created 3Doodler®, a 3D pen allowing artists to hand draw 3D objects.** Their two crowdfunding campaigns helped test the public's interest in their unique tool, leading not only to nearly $4 million in pledges, but the launch of a successful business.

➤ **Alice's dog Pepper has a serious, but treatable, medical condition that would result in a shortened lifespan without expensive surgery.** Alice's friends and family helped organize a crowdfunding campaign to raise the $5,000 necessary to cover Pepper's medical bills.

➤ **Jonathan wanted to create a large-scale, interactive art installation.** He crowdfunded Visualize Somerville, a multisensory, attendee-controlled art installation. This ephemeral experience allowed backers to not only support his project, but to also actively engage and become part of the creation itself.

➤ **Catherine, a songwriter and bandleader, had created a concept album celebrating historical and mythical women, but the project was incomplete.** She wanted to add a visual component to the project and had come up with the idea of producing a film anthology to accompany the songs. She raised money to hire 14 filmmakers from around the world to create the *Bring Us Your Women* film.

➤ **Every year, FamilyAid Boston sets up a crowdfunding campaign for volunteer runners taking part in the Boston Marathon.** Runners and their supporters solicit pledges that are used by the organization to help homeless families find housing. Last year, the campaign raised more than $100,000.

➤ **Alexandria turned to a crowdfunding patronage system to support her projects.** Backers pay a small amount of money at a regular interval, or when she creates something new. This allows her to focus on doing video and photo shoots to showcase her costume creations.

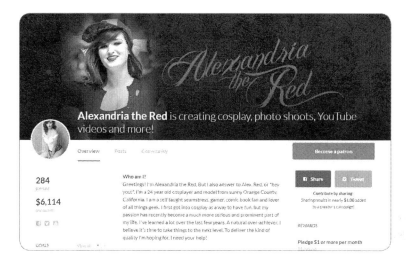

> **Roger was a journalist looking to write a historical piece about the use of certain technologies in Cold-War-era espionage.** There was great interest in the story from several publications and from the public, but his budget was too limited to thoroughly investigate without additional support. Roger raised money via crowdfunding to file Freedom of Information Act requests and to travel to primary sources to gather information for his story.

The scope and goals of these projects may have been different, but each one attracted a group of backers to help overcome financial and logistical hurdles to transform an otherwise impossible dream into a successful reality. Moreover, backers were empowered to be part of bringing the creator's ideas to fruition.

How can crowdfunding work for you?

Now that you have read a few success stories, you may be wondering if crowdfunding could work for your concept. This book will not only explain how crowdfunding works, it will also show the practical steps involved in running a campaign:

> In Chapter 1, we will examine the philosophical and logistical differences between crowdfunding and traditional funding, before breaking down the types of projects well-suited for crowdfunding efforts.

➤ Chapter 2 is all about planning, from choosing the right platform to setting up a realistic budget.

➤ Chapter 3 discusses the preparation of promotional materials and explains how to set up reward tiers for backers.

➤ In Chapter 4, we will explore communication tactics, including press outreach and methods for keeping backers engaged.

➤ Chapter 5 covers post-campaign activities, from keeping backers informed about the progress of your project to distributing rewards.

By the time we finish, you will be well on your way to running your own crowdfunding campaign. We only have 30 minutes, so let's get started!

CHAPTER 1

Why crowdfunding?

Imagine you are in a band, The Von Nerds. The group has written 15 songs, and is ready to make its first album. In the old days, you and the other band members might scrape together the cash to pay for a few days in a professional recording studio. But it would be risky—there is no easy way to estimate how many albums The Von Nerds could sell, or how much of the initial investment you could recoup through sales.

With crowdfunding, The Von Nerds has an opportunity to raise money and better understand fan support in advance of recording. It reduces financial risk, and helps to set a realistic estimate of available resources.

Many types of crowdfunding projects work in a similar way. In such cases, crowdfunding campaigns serve as presales of a product. They help gauge interest and reduce risk. Essentially, the campaigns let creators test the waters to determine if the interest is sufficient to cover start-up costs.

For creative projects such as music recordings, feedback from the crowdfunding campaign could help determine the budget for the total number of hours spent in the recording studio or the complexity of the final packaging of the product. In addition, presales can also ensure that the investment to create the first production run will be recouped and that manufacturers and others involved in the creative process can be guaranteed compensation.

For instance, if The Von Nerds manage to raise $7,000, that's enough to spend a week in the studio and print 500 copies of the disc with a 16-page, 4-color insert with photos and lyrics. If, however, the band only raises $3,000, they will only be able to spend two days in the studio and will have to settle for a black-and-white insert and a much smaller pressing.

Twenty or thirty years ago, businesses such as record labels or investors would front the money for efforts like these. The expectation was that the investors would own a portion of not just initial sales, but also of future profits. There was a tradeoff of financial risk for future reward. With a properly planned crowdfunding campaign, a much larger number of backers serve as investors, but their risk and reward is more limited.

Crowdfunding and investing laws

In the United States, securities laws have significantly restricted the ways in which crowdfunding backers can expect to earn a profit from their support. Instead of receiving a share of the company or a portion of future earnings, backers of crowdfunding projects typically receive non-financial rewards such as early access to the product itself. For other types of crowdfunding projects, special recognition, credit, or even just the satisfaction of backers knowing they are part of bringing an idea to fruition can be enough. Backers feel good about supporting their friends, family, and independent creators, and they know the outcome would not have been possible without their support.

While some venture capitalists use the term "crowdfunding" to refer to the microinvestment of capital in entrepreneurial projects with expected financial returns, in this book we will only discuss crowdfunding systems that are not based around an investment model. In other words, for all the project types mentioned here, backers will not receive any financial return or stake in a product. Many of the websites and crowdfunding platforms described in this book explicitly disallow campaign creators from offering investment opportunities, as these would fall under a stricter set of regulations, making them less accessible to average individuals with interesting project ideas. Indiegogo is an exception— the crowdfunding platform now gives entrepreneurs the option of offering equity to backers. Other platforms may soon follow.

The importance of being the underdog

Backers of crowdfunding projects often consider themselves to be part of a community coming together to bypass unfair economic systems and traditional gatekeepers. While large-scale, professionally organized crowdfunding projects exist, many backers believe crowdfunding campaigns should be used primarily by those without access to traditional sources of funding. Backers want to support the underdog, and may look down on founders with access to wealth or traditional investors.

Further, backers want to believe they are helping someone make his or her entrepreneurial or creative dream possible. They regard crowdfunding as a great equalizer, allowing wonderful ideas to come to life. For example, many people believe renewable energy sources are not receiving sufficient government or corporate investment and attention, so projects like Solar Roadways, an initiative to replace roads with solar panels that you can drive, park, and walk on, receive a lot of community attention. The project has attracted a great deal of support, and managed to raise over $2 million from more than 50,000 backers.

Crowdfunding philosophies: donations vs. sales

Backers typically think of projects as philosophically divided, partially or completely, between two categories: donations and sales.

Donation projects are designed to produce art, ideas, social or political movements, services, or public objects that backers believe should exist. Backers typically do not own the final product or outcome, but are satisfied that they could help ensure a worthy creation or specific outcome resulted from the campaign.

For donation campaigns, backers may receive some object commemorating their contribution—a thank-you note, an attribution, or a related piece of memorabilia, for example—but the primary outcome is not the object delivered to backers.

There are all kinds of donation-themed projects. I have contributed to charity campaigns including things like training a service dog for a young child with medical issues, bringing solar-powered water pumps to villages in Central America, and helping facilitate a return to school for young drop-outs in Kenya. Later in this chapter, we will look at several other types of crowdfunding projects that follow the donation philosophy.

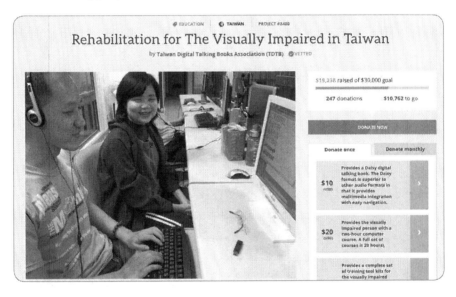

Sales projects seek to raise money to allow the design, manufacturing, and distribution of a physical good that backers desire to possess. Unlike going to a store and buying something that already exists, providing money in advance to a sales-based crowdfunding project enables the actual creation of the product. Advance purchases provide seed capital to cover costs of design and manufacturing that might otherwise be infeasible.

This form of crowdfunding provides a vote of confidence for the creation of innovative goods. I have backed crowdfunding campaigns to directly purchase new and innovative coffee pots, keychains, handbags, and camera gear before they were available for purchase through traditional retailers. Although some of these products later found commercial success through traditional retail channels, others did not.

Crowdfunding is not just about money

For creators, crowdfunding has the potential to address various project needs. Obviously, crowdfunding campaigns serve to collect money to make the idea economically possible, but the community benefits are arguably more significant. Project backers feel emotionally invested in the success of a project. This is true both during the fundraising campaign itself and when the project is brought to life.

Regardless of how a founder launches a creative or entrepreneurial project, one of the most challenging aspects of attaining success is finding an audience or customer base. Crowdfunding has a built-in advantage of establishing a community of enthusiastic supporters during the campaign. Once a backer has helped fund a project, he or she has status as an early adopter with bragging rights as a tastemaker or trailblazer. We all love to be the first to use or own a new technology, the first to see an exciting film, or even to be able to point out our name in the credits. Backing projects can raise the social status of the backers themselves. As a result, they have some personal investment in the external notoriety and recognition of the final product. This is especially rewarding when the project becomes successful outside of the backer community!

Such recognition has been a primary benefit of the crowdsourced film projects I have participated in. Once a film is released, it is not uncommon to see several hundred supporters spreading the word to their respective social circles, noting they have a "special thanks" in the credits. This type of enthusiasm and publicity can be very hard to obtain organically. In addition, people who back crowdfunded projects tend to be active and enthusiastic promoters of the things they love. These are the kinds of vocal and engaged tastemakers you want for your project!

A dedicated crowdfunding community can also serve as a signal to investors that a project could achieve real business success. Some entrepreneurs leverage crowdfunding as a proof-of-concept to raise larger pools of money via traditional methods. Investors certainly love great ideas, but great ideas with proof of success and a vocal support base of tastemakers are even better.

What kinds of projects are suitable?

So you have an idea for a new backpack that has a cool feature not previously seen in backpack technology: a system of zippers, flaps, and struts that converts the backpack into a small tent! You have been designing the backpack for years, and after making a prototype for your own use, your friends ask how they can get one just like it. In fact, you think it might be popular beyond your group of friends. The backpacks are not too expensive to make, but with one quick look at your bank account, you realize you can't afford to produce a large number of backpacks without additional funds.

The convertible backpack is the type of project that could be perfect for a crowdfunding campaign. Consider the following attributes:

➤ It's innovative and unique.

➤ There is a large potential audience or user base.

➤ To potential buyers, the product is worth more than it costs to make.

➤ You are passionate about it!

But innovative physical products are just one kind of project that is suitable for crowdfunding. Let's look at some of the other types of projects that might be a good fit for crowdfunding campaigns.

Creative

Creative projects involve the creation and usually public presentation of a specific piece of art, literature, music, or film. The creative work can be physical, such as a book or art installation, or it may be digital, like a sound recording. It may exist in a permanent form, or be a fleeting experience, lasting for just a single performance or showing. Backers usually receive physical or digital copies of the creations, or are invited to attend performances. It is also common for backers to receive recognition as patrons of the creators or the work via a written credit or some sort of acknowledgement.

Example: When poet and performer Jade Sylvan and director and dancer Fem Bones had the idea for *Spider Cult the Musical*, a B-movie musical, burlesque, and multimedia show with a live, original, rock score, the concept was immediately embraced by fans of the many artists involved. The blend of genres and formats brought together a diverse base of support. Some of the backers had never seen a burlesque show, while others had never seen a musical. The short run, performed two years after the campaign ran, involved more than 50 artists and opened to rave reviews.

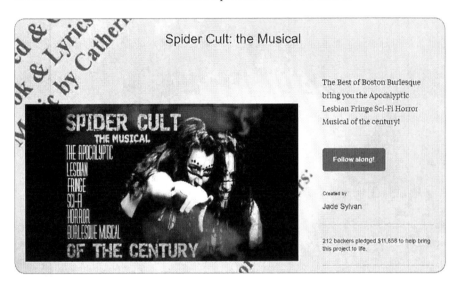

Spider Cult: the Musical

The Best of Boston Burlesque bring you the Apocalyptic Lesbian Fringe Sci-Fi Horror Musical of the century!

Follow along!

Created by
Jade Sylvan

212 backers pledged $11,858 to help bring this project to life.

Entrepreneurial

Entrepreneurial projects focus on the creation of goods and services that have commercial appeal. Examples include clothing and accessories, mechanical or electronic devices, and software, similar to what might otherwise be purchased in a store or via an online retailer. Backers often gain early access to ownership of the product if and when it enters production.

Example: Daniel had an idea for a camera attachment that made focusing and zooming easier and more ergonomic. The LensShifter campaign was popular with videographers, photographers, and interested amateurs who desired enhanced precision for their lenses. Their backing allowed Daniel and Engineerable to mass-produce this innovative product.

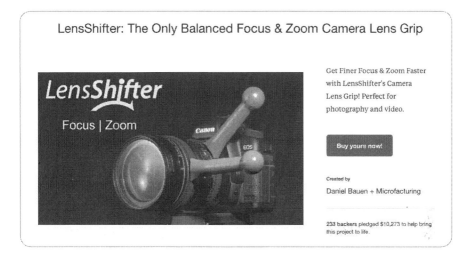

Public good/charity

Public good/charity projects are used to conduct an activity or create objects that serve the public in some way. Backers may receive recognition, but typically do not receive special access. Such projects cover a broad range of possibilities, but could include the installation of public art or monuments, the founding of a library, or the creation of an afterschool music program. Backers often provide donations because they believe an underserved community or organization will be helped by the projects. The campaigns may also include various rewards that drive contributions, such as T-shirts or tote bags.

Example: Michele was responsible for running a local film casting and connections website, NewEnglandFilm.com, but there were several new features that could help the site better serve the community. Michele wanted to hire a web programmer to fund development of the features. She found crowdfunding support from the existing user community to help grow the scope and usefulness of the site .

Individual support

Individual support projects are another type of charity project, but serve to help an individual or family with a pressing financial issue. These are most frequently associated with unexpected medical expenses or emergency financial situations such as foreclosures. Some campaigns are focused on individual growth by raising money for college tuition, specialized job training, or access to transportation.

Patronage

Patronage projects follow a well-established historical model to support creative and individual projects. Throughout history, a range of prominent artists, including Michelangelo, Beethoven, and Renoir have relied on the patronage of wealthy individuals and organizations to pay for their living expenses so they could fully devote themselves to their art. Crowdfunded patronage projects serve a similar purpose. They typically involve recurring payments to individuals who receive support based on their track records rather than what they have specifically proposed to create. The assumption is that funding living costs for artists will allow them to continue to create, and that backers will find those future creations compelling.

While there is usually a vague outline of future creative work attached to a campaign to attract contributions, patronage projects do not come with a promise of a specific outcome between creators and backers. Creators are just implicitly trusted by backers to continue down their current creative path. It is typical in these campaigns for backers to receive special additional benefits for contributing, such as access to behind-the-scenes materials or exclusive content.

Example: Animal Wonders is a Patreon-funded YouTube channel providing fun and educational information about animals along with a behind-the-scenes look at caring for over 80 exotic animals.

Mixed

Some projects may straddle different crowdfunding categories. In such cases, backers are attracted by a combination of rewards and specific outcomes. One of my favorite examples is Parts and Crafts, a family makerspace and community workshop. In 2011, the organizers ran a Kickstarter campaign in which backers would receive a kit to make a lightsaber. For every backer sale, money would go to support a sliding scale, scholarships, and outreach efforts for maker programs for local children. More than five years later, Parts and Crafts is an established nonprofit organization, and is still going strong in its community!

CHAPTER 2

Planning the campaign

Now that you have decided crowdfunding is right for your project, it is time to go through the process of designing your campaign and choosing the right platform. Undoubtedly, your idea is innovative, exciting, and very important to you. However, to attract support, you really have to stand out. The design and planning decisions you make now will directly impact how much of a potential backer's time and attention you can hope to garner. More importantly, your approach will determine how many people you will be able to convert to actual backers of your campaign.

Think of it as a three-step process:

1. Engage their curiosity.

2. Present a clear, concise, and compelling narrative that makes them want to get involved.

3. Formalize the relationship by getting them to sign up as backers and pledge their support.

It is common for backers to visit your campaign two, three, four, or even five times before finally making a pledge. Some backers are waiting until they get a paycheck at work before they commit to backing the campaign. Others are on the fence, unable to decide whether to get involved. Some procrastinators will put off making a decision until the final days of your campaign. As we will see later in the book, plan on sustained work to successfully convert casual browsers to committed backers.

Choosing the right platform

Before getting started, you will need to choose the appropriate platform for your project. What matters when choosing a crowdfunding platform? Here are a few factors that may influence your decision:

➤ **Is it appropriate?** If you want to bring to life that convertible backpack we discussed at the beginning of this chapter, then a platform that supports entrepreneurial goals is more appropriate than a public good/charity-focused platform.

➤ **Technical considerations.** Will the platform allow you to upload the materials you consider best for your project? For instance, if you plan on making a high-quality video to promote your campaign, then the platform must support video uploads. Check FAQs and support resources to determine what's technically feasible on a specific platform.

➤ **Logistical factors.** Is the platform available in your country, or a country in which potential supporters may be concentrated? Does it support running a campaign for the duration you have chosen? Does it allow your selected funding model? Don't assume anything—choosing the wrong platform could spell disaster for your campaign if supporters can't participate!

Below, we will look at the various types of campaigns commonly encountered on crowdfunding sites, as well as specific sites that focus on a certain niche.

All-or-nothing systems for creative or entrepreneurial projects (Kickstarter)

All-or-nothing crowdfunding systems are based on fixed funding goals. A creator will only receive the money if the target is met while the campaign is running. In other words, if the creator sets a goal of $10,000 but only receives pledges for $9,902 before the campaign deadline, he or she won't receive a cent.

This may sound harsh, but I believe it is a strong motivator for contributors to help creators reach their targets. In addition, pledges that exceed the goal will be passed on to the creator. So, if the creator sets a target of $10,000 and receives $11,000 in pledges before the deadline, he or she will receive $11,000 (minus associated site fees).

Kickstarter is not only the most popular all-or-nothing crowdfunding site, but it's also the most popular crowdfunding site overall. The term "Kickstarter" has become synonymous with crowdfunding campaigns in general, and backers supporting campaigns on other sites will often describe them as "Kickstarter campaigns." Because Kickstarter is such a commonly recognized brand, it often houses the most publicized and successful creative and entrepreneurial campaigns.

Name recognition and market dominance have made Kickstarter's funding system widely accepted among backers. Kickstarter claims it has helped creators raise more than $3 billion dollars across more than 120,000 crowdfunding projects. More than ⅓ of Kickstarter projects have ended up successfully funded, meaning that they reached their all-or-nothing goal. The majority of successful campaigns raised between $1,000 and $10,000. Backers are often quite focused on rewards, more so than on many other sites.

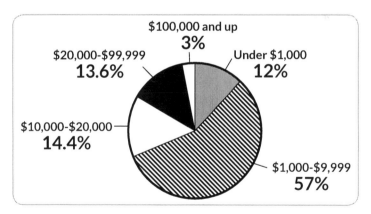

You may suppose all-or-nothing sounds like a big commitment and it would be safer to use a different system in which you could receive pledges even if the goal was not met. There is, however, an extremely useful psychological component to an all-or-nothing crowdfunding campaign. It relates to the campaign budget.

Let's say you are planning to crowdfund your convertible backpack idea from Chapter 1, and have a budget associated with it—$20,000 to move from prototype to limited production, including rewards and overhead (these topics will be discussed later in the book). If you want to complete the project as outlined, it is necessary to raise at least $20,000. If you can complete the project with less money, your goal has not been appropriately set, and potential backers will be reluctant to participate in your campaign. In an all-or-nothing campaign, you are really saying the project will only be possible if the goal is met. Backers will then feel a special value in their contribution. They are bringing the otherwise impossible to life. Campaigns that do not require full funding to complete are inherently carrying the idea that the money is not all that necessary for the project to move forward.

There is another psychological component at work. No one wants to be part of a losing campaign. That means that once a backer has contributed, he or she will feel like they are part of the team and will help spread the word about the campaign to other potential backers to ensure its success. In fact, backers who have already pledged and see a campaign underperforming will often increase their pledge amounts to help build momentum during tough periods.

Partial-funding systems for creative or entrepreneurial projects (Indiegogo)

Partial-funding systems include a goal, but any money raised during the campaign will be delivered to the creator even if the goal is not met. In other words, if the creator sets a goal of $10,000 but only receives pledges for $9,902 before the deadline, he or she will still receive $9,902 (minus associated site fees).

Example: All-or-nothing vs. partial funding ($10,000 goal).

Model	Pledges	Amount raised
All-or-nothing	$9,902	$0
Partial funding	$9,902	$9,902 (minus site fees)

It may seem like a no-brainer to go the partial-funding route. However, I generally advise against using a partial-funding goal unless you believe it to be absolutely necessary. While there are no public data on outcomes, I believe partial-funding campaigns consistently raise less money overall than they would using all-or-nothing campaigns. Contributors do not feel the same urgency to commit to the project, and are less concerned about the project's failure—after all, the campaign organizers will at least get something.

Falling short of the goal can lead to other problems. I have contributed to several campaigns that missed the stated goal by a very high percentage. One film I contributed to using a partial-funding site set a goal of $20,000, but only raised $500. At the end of the campaign, the creators had $500, but they also had to deal with backers' expectations that they would be able to complete the $20,000 film they promised to them in their campaign description. Their options at that point included refunding pledges or finding another way to fund the project.

Indiegogo is the most popular partial-funding crowdfunding site. It's worth noting that Indiegogo also allows all-or-nothing campaigns. Campaign creators with creative and entrepreneurial projects often go to Indiegogo for their campaigns when the all-or-nothing Kickstarter model seems too daunting or the campaign outcomes are less predictable. Indiegogo varies its fees based on whether the funding goal was met or not.

Presale systems for creative projects (PledgeMusic)

A presale crowdfunding website is kind of like a store. Backers are making purchases very early in the process, and are actually helping to facilitate the creation of the project itself.

For instance, PledgeMusic lets creators focus on presales of items and experiences, generally associated with a single project. It also allows for a la carte add-ons of rewards. In fact, PledgeMusic refers to a fundraising campaign as a "store," and pledges as "pre-orders" of items.

Project-resource systems for creative projects (Seed&Spark)

Seed&Spark requires creators to break down their projects into very specific, itemized budgets. Backers can either pledge money to pay for specific parts of the budget, or can provide the items themselves.

For example, a project on Seed&Spark may require a truck to move materials from one site to another. A potential backer may own a truck and pledge use of the vehicle to the campaign, rather than giving money to cover the truck rental cost.

Patronage systems (Patreon)

Patronage is the financial or other support given by an individual or organization to an artist or other creator. It is a longstanding historical practice in which royalty, religious organizations, and wealthy families paid artists' living expenses and provided access and opportunities.

Examples abound. The Roman poets Horace and Virgil were supported by Gaius Maecenas. Leonardo Da Vinci's patron was Isabella D'Este, while Shakespeare received support from Queen Elizabeth.

Patronage-based crowdfunding is a system of ongoing support for artists. However, instead of a single rich person or guild providing funds, a group of individuals make pledges of varying amounts on an ongoing basis. The following fictional example lists supporters of a new patronage-based crowdfunding campaign to support a website promoting music education for school-aged children. The support hasn't reached the level sought by organizers, but it's a good start considering only four people have signed up so far:

Example: Patronage-supported music education website ($1,000 monthly goal).

Patron	Monthly pledge	Percentage of goal
Hector Desouza	$50	5%
Charlene Grinnell	$150	15%
Terry Nesbitt	$10	1%
Penelope Lee	$50	5%
Total	$260	26%

Patreon is the most popular site to provide an ongoing-support model of crowdfunding. Patreon creators are generally producing regular content on a smaller scale rather than occasional, large-scale projects. As such, it would be difficult to run regular crowdfunding campaigns to cover each small project. A patronage-based system allows backers to recognize that the ongoing work of a creator is valuable and to pledge money at a regular interval, typically monthly, to help the creator continue. This reduces the time spent by the creator on planning and running crowdfunding campaigns. Generally, in exchange for these pledges, backers receive exclusive content or early access.

Patreon also lets backers choose to make contributions upon the release of a specific creation. So, for example, if I ran a Patreon campaign for a podcast, backers could elect to make an automatic contribution each time an episode is released.

Individual support (GoFundMe)

Crowdfunding sites focused on the support of individuals are very common. You may have been invited to such a site to help someone go to college, pay for a medical emergency, or cover other expenses that the individual would otherwise be unable to pay for. Backers are not motivated by rewards or other benefits associated with some of the campaign types described earlier. In that sense, standard crowdfunding principles do not apply.

GoFundMe is a popular site for raising money for individual needs. Most often, these include unexpected medical expenses such as hospital stays, surgery, medical equipment, and other health interventions that exceed insurance benefits.

Public good/charity (GlobalGiving)

This category probably offers the most choices for people interested in raising money for important causes. There are many viable platforms that host projects ranging from hurricane relief to coral preservation to supporting rural schools.

As these are charitable causes and donations are tax-deductible in the United States, many standard principles of crowdfunding will not apply. Rewards are seldom offered. Instead, giving tiers are specified by impact ("$100 will buy 6 school desks for children").

GlobalGiving is one of many sites that support traditional charitable cause campaigns. The site attempts to connect international nonprofits with donors and corporate partners. One of the benefits of the site is that it performs significant work vetting nonprofits to determine that they are using money collected from backers as presented. GlobalGiving also offers matching campaigns and bonus prizes to help motivate backers.

Time, budget, and legal considerations

Of the some 500 projects I have personally backed, nearly 100 failed to complete the project to specifications and/or failed to deliver rewards. In addition, more than 300 delivered rewards later than the dates specified. Nevertheless, I don't believe the people running these campaigns intended to carry out fraud. As someone who has launched many campaigns, I am all too aware that projects are nearly always more complex than creators expect. All kinds of unanticipated problems can arise that undermine plans and budgets.

Although crowdfunding sites are taking action to reduce the number of campaigns that do not deliver, experienced backers will want to see sufficient evidence of proper budgeting and contingency planning. The slightest whiff of unprofessionalism in the campaign materials will deter potential backers and seed doubt in the ability of the creator to execute the campaign.

Time requirements: longer than you think!

Whenever I work with people who are new to crowdfunding, the first thing I tell them is whatever amount of time they have in mind to create and run their campaigns, it will probably take twice or even three times that long to be successful. It is simply not enough to have a great idea, present it to the world, and sit back and let the money roll in. Crowdfunding campaigns require meticulous planning, constant attention, and a robust adaptability. You not only have to be at the top of your game to handle the inevitable surprises, but you also have to keep up the effort during the fulfillment period, which may last for months after the campaign formally ends.

Later, we will outline the specifics of the design and operation of a crowdfunding campaign. In general, I tell people to expect to spend between 40 and 60 hours preparing their campaign, and an additional 20 hours per week during the campaign. There will be additional tasks after the campaign ends, including communicating with backers and distributing rewards. It is certainly possible to outsource tasks to PR firms or virtual assistants to reduce the time requirements. But for many types of campaigns, backers really want to feel a direct connection with the creator of the campaign. They will not necessarily respond the same way to copy created by a public relations firm as they would a heartfelt message from the creator or a member of the core team.

Example: Time commitment for campaign-related tasks

Pre-campaign	Week 1	Week 2	Week 3	Post-campaign	Total
50 hours	23 hours	15 hours	20 hours	60 hours	168 hours

When running a campaign, you should expect to set aside time each day to communicate with backers and media. You will also have to devote time to answering questions from potential backers.

Before beginning your campaign, you will want to create a calendar assigning planning and preparations for the campaign. This calendar should include a timeline for creating video, photos, and other assets that you will need for the campaign. I typically create this calendar using both Google Calendar and spreadsheet software such as Google Sheets. Time will need to be budgeted to ensure that descriptions and marketing copy is written, technical elements are in place, and your campaign can be reviewed by trusted friends and experts.

Crowdfunding sites usually allow organizers to work on campaigns in draft mode. This means you can build your campaign in stages, adding content as it's completed. Once the campaign is in a near-final state, you can send a private link to select viewers to ask whether your ideas are clearly presented, your narrative is sufficiently compelling, and your rewards are enticing. While you may be itching to get your campaign out in the public eye as soon as possible, it is best to go live when you are truly ready—some potential backers will only be willing to read your campaign description once before making a decision.

Finally, a common pitfall for creators is to underestimate the time and money required to produce rich media for the campaign, including the all-important campaign video. We will discuss the production of multimedia content in Chapter 3.

Creating an accurate crowdfunding budget

Budgets are essential to both the internal workings of your team, as well as the public face of your crowdfunding campaign. Backers prefer to know what their contributions are paying for, and that individual contributions allow for something essential to happen in the context of the project.

Some crowdfunding sites operate like wedding registries. Seed&Spark, a project-resource system discussed earlier, encourages contributions based on very specific budgetary needs. It also allows the donation of goods and services to cover line items in lieu of cash.

Other sites allow accumulated funds to be spent at the discretion of the campaign organizer. The budget is not a contract, but rather a rough guide. For instance, Kickstarter does not explicitly require detailed budgets or backing levels that are tied to specific line items in a budget. Nevertheless, campaigns that show a reasonable and thoughtfully planned out budget can be more successful than those with vague or uncertain budgets.

For creative and entrepreneurial projects, backers vastly prefer campaigns in which no money goes directly into the pockets of campaign creators. To some extent, even in the case of the most traditionally business-oriented projects, backers see all crowdfunding as charitable giving. Crowdsourcing is often associated with charities, which not only raise funds from small and large donors, but also employ pledge-reward systems to encourage giving at specific levels. Just as people look down at charities that don't spend their money wisely, crowdfunding backers also frown on nonessential overhead costs, such as salaries. If you do decide to include such costs in your budget, you must give the appropriate context and justification, but even then, many backers will be skeptical.

When I am working on a campaign, I try to keep the budget short and simple. Categories, costs, and explanations are clearly explained. Here's the budget breakdown for a recent vampire film:

Item	Est. cost	Notes
Cast	$5,000	The largest cast we have ever worked with (>25 actors).
Crew	$3,000	Hiring makeup, hair, artwork, sound, and camera assistants.
Food	$2,000	We want to make sure our cast and crew are well fed!
Wardrobe	$2,000	Vintage clothing supplemented with custom-made items.
Props	$1,000	Items include stakes, crossbows, candelabras, etc.
Location rentals & insurance	$2,000	City requires liability insurance for exclusive use of a public space.
Film festivals	$3,000	Covers submissions and materials to film festivals.
Rewards	$12,000	Production and delivery.
Kickstarter fees	$3,000	In the U.S., Kickstarter charges 5% + payment processing fees (3%–5%)

The costs for the film totaled some $33,000. An entrepreneurial budget breakdown for a coffee-table book might be similarly expensive, although many budget line items will be different:

Editor	$2,000
Book designer	$5,000
Printing	$15,000
Reward shipping	$3,000
Website creation and hosting	$2,000
Kickstarter fees	$3,000

One of the greatest challenges in budgeting is predicting overhead costs for a campaign. When designing rewards, it's not hard to determine the final yield from a campaign after the associated rewards overhead has been subtracted. The problem comes in estimating the portion of backers choosing each reward level. We will discuss reward tiers later in the book.

How much can you raise?

When creating a campaign, be realistic about milestones and the ultimate funding goal. Fundraising experts often cite 30% as a base for a new campaign. In crowdfunding terms, you should be confident that upon launching your campaign, you will be able to raise approximately 30% of your goal within the first five days. Very often, the first 30% will come from close friends, family, and any existing fans or supporters from previous campaigns or other activities.

It's not hard to estimate what 30% would equal. Simply ask friends, family, and other supporters if they would be willing to contribute once you launch. Your request should explain that you are looking for soft, uncommitted pledges with specified contribution amounts, and that once you pull the trigger on the campaign, they will formally back the campaign within a few days. Sum these soft commitments to estimate where your 30% target lies.

If you are running an all-or-nothing campaign on a site like Kickstarter, avoid setting too high a goal. Your 30% estimate will give you a pretty good sense of where your campaign could end up. To leave a little margin, I recommend tripling your 30% amount and setting your all-or-nothing campaign goal on Kickstarter at 90% of your "true" goal. This gives you a 10% safety buffer and means that even if you fall slightly short of your true goal, you will still get the money from the campaign. If you set your true goal at a reasonable level, even if you only receive 90% of the true amount, you can still make the project work. If your estimate of what you can raise is not enough to complete your project, you will likely need to seek additional sources of funding to supplement your crowdfunding campaign.

Let's say you're setting up a Kickstarter campaign to prototype a new bicycle lock. Based on your analysis of the design, manufacturing, quality control, and delivery requirements, you determine the true goal to be $20,000. This means you are expecting friends and family to kick in $6,000 in the first five days, while your official all-or-nothing campaign goal on Kickstarter is $18,000.

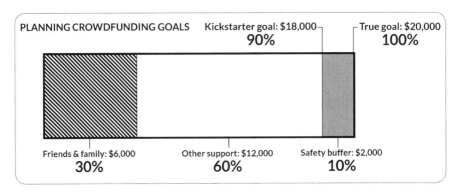

According to Kickstarter's statistics, more than half of successful campaigns exceed their stated goal by at least 10%, which gives campaign organizers some extra breathing room to reach their stated goals. For the bicycle lock campaign, you have about a 50% chance of ending up with pledges very close to (or exceeding) your true goal of $20,000. Campaigns I have been involved with have exceeded campaign goals by margins ranging from 9% to 54%. Remember, for all-or-nothing campaigns on Kickstarter and similar sites, you will not receive any money unless you meet 100% of your official goal.

When your campaign launches, be sure to quickly transform those soft pledges into recorded commitments on the crowdfunding website. This will ensure visitors to your campaign page will see early momentum and will be encouraged to take part in what will probably be a successful campaign. Another encouraging statistic from Kickstarter states that 81% of campaigns that receive 20% funding are ultimately successful. Campaigns jumping to 20–30% of the goal within the first few days look very attractive to potential backers. Later, we will look at how campaigns typically progress.

Campaign validation and stretch goals

Campaigns with little or no early pledges do not demonstrate public validation. This also leads to a negative feedback loop—even if potential backers are interested in the idea, they will be reluctant to make a public pledge to back an unpopular campaign for fear of looking foolish.

There is another angle to consider as well. Solid early momentum is extremely useful when seeking press of any kind. Campaigns with pledges out of the gate look hot and exciting and make for great media stories. The campaigns with crickets are unlikely to be covered by media outlets.

Crowdfunding sites tend to disallow the adjustment of goals once a campaign is launched. It is therefore essential that goals are set appropriately based on both the amount of money that can be realistically raised and the amount of money necessary to complete the project. However, there are many types of cost surprises that can pop up, which may require some adjustments on your part.

For instance, if the funding goal is met prior to the end of the campaign, you will likely still want more backers to contribute. One of the common approaches to motivating backers after the goal is reached is to offer "stretch goals" to explain how additional money will be used. These are typically written as expanded budget items and could include things like:

➤ Choice of extra colors for manufactured products.

➤ Additional songs for album recordings.

➤ A camera upgrade or better props for a film shoot.

The idea is to show that additional money will still be useful and help with the quality of the outcome of the project.

How long should your campaign run?

You may suppose that a long campaign will provide lots of time to raise money and find an audience. However, crowdfunding sites and experienced organizers recommend running relatively short campaigns of one month or less. Their reasoning: After a short while, most organizers start to feel burned out trying to maintain excitement and generate new content for long campaigns. According to Kickstarter, campaigns that are 30 days or less have higher success rates than longer campaigns. Indiegogo's analysis of 100,000 campaigns came to the same conclusion, noting that 30-day campaigns work best. Over $\frac{1}{3}$ of submitted projects that Kickstarter approves are successfully funded.

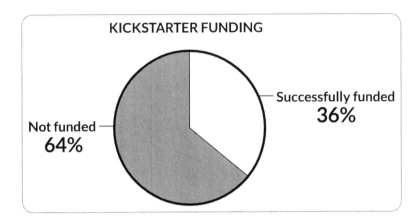

Hidden costs, from shipping to "backer melt"

It is important to remember that your goal must include money to cover campaign and fulfillment costs. It is very common for first-time crowd-funders to vastly underestimate these costs or fail to include a buffer for unexpected changes.

For one campaign I worked on, we calculated our reward shipping costs based on U.S. shipping rates. We assumed that only a few international backers would find the project compelling, and even if there were some overseas backers, we could turn to relatively inexpensive fixed-rate boxes to ship foreign packages.

We were wrong. It turned out a significant percentage of our backers lived overseas and during the year between the launch of the campaign and the fulfillment of rewards, the U.S. Postal Service dropped their fixed-rate air-mail box and replaced it with a service that was far more expensive.

Based on my experience with smaller creative campaigns, approximately 50% of the official goal will be taken up by campaign materials prep (which includes costs associated with producing video, photos, etc.), post-funding melt, site and transaction fees, and costs related to reward fulfillment. So, if we raise $30,000 on a project, we expect that only $15,000 of that will actu-ally go directly to the project itself. For a larger campaign, these costs will be proportionally lower, but still quite significant. For instance, a project raising $100,000 might lose $30,000 to overhead costs.

Organizers of crowdfunding campaigns should attempt to make clear estimates of overhead costs in the planning stages of a project. Unfortunately,
it's not easy to get the estimate right. While I have worked on many projects
that underestimated overhead, I have never worked on a project that budgeted too much to cover overhead costs. Regardless of how conservative the
estimates are, surprise costs always seem to pop up.

Numbers will vary somewhat depending on the specifics of a campaign, but
one sample breakdown for creators who can prepare their own materials
might look like this:

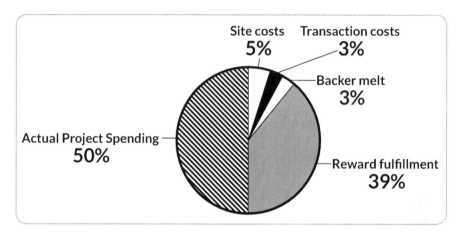

Site costs (5%): Crowdfunding sites typically operate by taking a cut of the
money raised during a campaign. The usual rate is 5%.

Transaction costs (3%): In addition to the 5% site fee for using a particular
crowdfunding system, there is typically a fee for credit card transactions
associated with the payments from backers. This averages approximately 3%.

Backer melt (3%): On many crowdfunding sites, backers make pledges and
associate a payment method with the pledge, but do not make the actual
payment until the campaign has ended. A small percentage of backers will
inevitably generate failed credit card transactions. It is worthwhile to personally reach out to backers whose payments have failed to see if there is a
way to reconcile the situation. Backer melt averages about 3% for most campaigns I have been a part of, but I have worked on a few campaigns that have
lost a single major backer who accounted for as much as 10% of all pledges.

Reward fulfillment: Fulfilling rewards will comprise the biggest overhead cost. Unfortunately, this category is often the hardest to accurately estimate. For some campaigns, the goal is to simply break even on providing rewards, and as such, fulfillment may consume as much as 80% of the money raised.

More than once I have backed entrepreneurial projects that budgeted for manufacturing processes. Lots of problems cropped up. Even when the team was able to put together a perfect prototype, the shift to mass production often led to unforeseen issues with materials or assembly. Several campaigns received quotes from overseas manufacturing facilities and found that once the money had been sent, production was not done correctly or at the quoted cost. In one case, an overseas manufacturer simply stole the design and began producing the product themselves without fulfilling the initial order.

In all, I have backed about 10 campaigns in which the cost of reward fulfillment exceeded the money raised by up to five times the original crowdfunding goal. As you might imagine, this created tremendous difficulties. Some campaigns were abandoned without fulfilling promises to backers. Others were forced to sell some inventory at a higher price to raise money to give backers their promised rewards.

It's a terrible feeling when you realize there is a major problem with rewards. For one of our film projects, we ordered DVDs of the final cut for backers and only discovered after shipping them out that the run was defective due to an error on our part. So we had to pay for a new batch of DVDs and a second round of shipping. This was a mistake that we should not have made, but these types of mistakes are surprisingly common when newbies deal with manufacturing and large-scale reward fulfillment for the first time.

Taxes and legal requirements

Taxes are another issue to watch out for. Not only do you have to follow all relevant tax laws, but it's also up to you to handle fundraising and expenditures in the most tax-efficient ways possible. Check with a lawyer or accountant before starting a campaign to ensure that you have planned correctly.

What sorts of problems crop up when it comes to crowdfunding and taxes? A friend of mine ran a campaign that raised $50,000 in December of one year. His intention was to spend the money on production costs the following year. However, he had not sought proper tax advice and ended up having to pay income tax on the $50,000 during the first year, and could only partially recover the money the following year after using the funds to pay for production. All told, he lost about $10,000 in taxes, a problem that could have largely been avoided had he run the campaign and spent the money in the same year.

In addition to complying with relevant tax codes, organizers of crowdfunding campaigns must also follow rules associated with specific platforms, not to mention laws and regulations established by municipal, state, and federal authorities. As crowdfunding grows, regulators have made it clear they will not tolerate theft, fraud, or violations of consumer protection statutes.

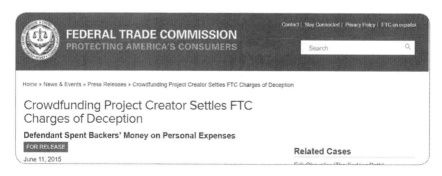

In recent years, investigators have filed charges against organizers of crowdfunding campaigns to raise money for bogus health emergencies and nonexistent products. GoFundMe has cancelled campaigns to raise money for questionable charities as well as people accused of serious crimes. Kickstarter has even hired an "integrity specialist" to cut down on nonsensical or unrealistic projects as well as outright scams.

Bottom line: As the organizer of a crowdfunding campaign, it's up to you to know your responsibilities and follow all relevant laws and regulations.

CHAPTER 3

Preparing campaign assets and rewards

Your campaign is a concise presentation of your story and your enthusiasm. Ultimately, the campaign must show that your project is exciting, unique, and worthy of their time.

For a new campaign, the major crowdfunding websites are structured to feature the following elements:

➤ A single logo image.

➤ A single video.

➤ Text descriptions and updates.

➤ Additional embedded content such as photos and audio clips.

No matter what category of crowdfunding campaign you are launching, it is extremely important to present content in a way that immediately gives potential backers an impression of professional expertise and trustworthiness. Crowdfunding campaigns are rarely guaranteed or formally endorsed by the sites themselves, so backers will evaluate the presentation of information to determine whether the project creator—you—can be trusted to keep your word and deliver rewards.

Unprofessional campaign assets could include:

➤ Spelling and grammar mistakes in the title or description.

➤ Brief or vague descriptions.

➤ Failure to show sufficient research and understanding of how the project will work.

➤ Low-resolution images.

➤ Poorly shot video.

➤ Video with bad audio.

➤ Photos and other content borrowed from commercial websites or from other creators who have not given permission.

➤ Poor eye contact in video.

➤ Very little information about the creator.

➤ Rewards that are not well explained or are inappropriately priced.

➤ An implausible or unclear budget and spending plan.

In essence, campaign descriptions must be well-written, concise, and typo-free. Videos and images should be professionally produced. When it comes to assessing trustworthiness of a campaign creator, backers will place quite a lot of value on how information is presented in the video and image content. You should expect to put a lot of time and energy into getting your presentation just right!

Moreover, for many types of campaigns, it is extremely important to have the right kinds of rewards that not only deliver real value to backers, but also won't eat up your budget. Well-designed reward tiers can attract more interest and help you reach your campaign goals.

Telling your story with video, images, and text

Images are the first things to jump out to potential backers when they look at a crowdfunding campaign. Countless studies have shown that we all extract a tremendous amount of information from images alone. Most people can't help but look at photos or illustrations when presented with them.

Naturally, the tone and content of your images must match the tone and content of the campaign. In addition, your images need to look like they were competently acquired, edited, and presented. If you have the budget or connections, I highly recommend working with professional photographers and videographers to present a slick, clear message for your campaign. One of the biggest mistakes made by first-time creators is uploading low-quality video content made with their phones. Creators who do this wrongly assume their enthusiasm and the quality of their ideas will make up for the unprofessional presentation on crowdfunding websites.

There are other common video mistakes made by first-time crowdfunders, including assuming that a video should tell the whole story of the campaign and answer all possible questions. This approach is ineffective—not as many backers will stick around to watch a video longer than 2 minutes. In fact, according to data from Wistia, as video duration gets longer, retention gets worse (see graph, below). Thus, I recommend presenting the main concept within the first 20 seconds of your video and telling your whole story in less than 90 seconds.

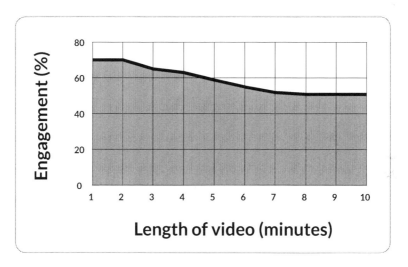

Here are additional guidelines for campaign videos:

➤ Short and concise is better than long and wordy.

➤ Take time to be clear about the project, but be succinct.

➤ Explain the critical nature of the project.

➤ Explain why crowdfunding is necessary to complete the project.

➤ End with a call to action—specifically, a request to get involved by pledging support or taking some other important action.

Keep in mind that potential backers view crowdfunding as helping ordinary people succeed in their dreams. So, while it is extremely useful for a video to look professional, it is also critical to present a personal story. You, the campaign organizer, should appear in the video to tell your story, and you should do so in a friendly, relatable manner. Backers will want to join a campaign because they are rooting for you to succeed!

In terms of structure, here is a basic format to follow:

1. Make a brief personal introduction (5 seconds).

2. Give a quick overview of the campaign (15 seconds).

3. Present various selling points and campaign requirements (60 seconds). This section should convince potential backers that the campaign is something they would like to be involved in. As we will discuss in the rewards section, the more a campaign is centered around creating a community (as opposed to creating a product), the more backers will want to get involved.

4. The video should close with a heartfelt plea to take action and join the campaign (10 seconds).

Michael J. Epstein
Writer / Director

Sophia Cacciola
Writer / Director

The above still from one of our Kickstarter videos shows our attempt to capture our individual personalities as well as the style of the film. We used a visual arrangement similar to the type of film we planned to make, lit the scene like our proposed film, and presented props that were slated to appear in the film. These cues helped convey the film's look and style to the audience while trying to keep us personable. We had to make decisions about how to style ourselves, how to dress, and how to talk with each other and the audience to remain engaging. There are many factors to consider. For each project, different options will appeal depending on the nature of the campaign and the character of the team.

Ten tips for creating a great video

Based on my own experience producing campaign videos and helping others to create effective video assets, here are some important tips:

1. Write a script and practice what you are going to say. Recording a compelling video presentation is far harder than most people think. It may require many takes, but getting it right is worth it.

2. Use images, lighting, coloring, music, and visual composition that match the tone of your project. You want to create emotion that matches the project presentation.

3. Dress up, smile, and be enthusiastic!

4. Be sure that images and music are properly licensed. While some people assume that the legal doctrine known as Fair Use trumps standard copyright law, it rarely applies to crowdfunding videos. Practically speaking, this means you cannot use your favorite pop hit as the background music for your campaign video. If you need royalty-free music, images, or other content, there are numerous stock websites that offer free or low-cost material.

5. Shoot your video in a wide-aspect ratio (16:9 or 2.35:1), which looks modern and conveys a more professional quality to the video.

6. Shoot your video in high-definition (HD) or Ultra HD formats. Many sites will shrink campaign videos to a lower resolution, but even when downscaled, HD video will almost always result in a final product with better color and detail than the older standard-definition (SD) format.

7. Record sound using an external microphone, such as a boom microphone or a lavalier microphone that clips to subjects' shirts or jackets. Built-in camera microphones not only have terrible sound quality, but are also regarded as the mark of amateurs and will immediately

give the impression of an unprofessional campaign. In fact, if you must choose between focusing on high-quality sound or high-quality video, sound should come first.

8. Make sure you have someone do a proper sound mix. Sound levels should be balanced and equalized, speech needs to sit comfortably above any background music, and there should be no distortion.

9. Edit video with professional-grade software. Pay close attention to the specifications provided for video uploads and ensure that your video is output in the highest resolution, best format, and at the highest bitrate allowed by those specifications.

10. Make sure the editing of video clips creates a feeling of high energy and movement.

For most people, these tips require turning to professionals who know how to handle video recording, sound recording, lighting, music production, sound mixing, editing, and post-production. Hiring experienced pros can be expensive, but you also need to keep an eye on your overall budget. If you are trying to raise $1,000, you cannot spend $5,000 producing professional visuals. Most potential backers will understand this. However, campaigns with bigger goals are expected to follow different standards. Failing to meet those expectations could prove to be a disaster.

Perfecting the written pitch

In addition to creating a campaign video, organizers of a new campaign will also have to prepare text that will appear on the description to entice potential backers. While a written pitch appearing next to a campaign video may seem redundant, the text can include more information for the overview and can also provide a detailed breakdown of the project.

When I write copy for campaigns, I always assume that for every additional paragraph I add, about 20% of potential backers will stop reading. While 100% might read the first paragraph, only 80% will continue to the second. By the fourth paragraph, I have already lost about half of my audience. If they have to scroll further to continue reading, only a few potential backers will be left by the time they get to the bottom of the page.

Therefore, it is critical to quickly convey your main ideas. Ideally, some potential backers will want to sign up as soon as they read the overview and watch the video. For people who are still on the fence, present an expansion of details as the text continues. For those readers who still want to learn more, I often write several screens of text to satisfy their curiosity. It is not a problem that other readers have stopped earlier so long as they have been presented with the essence of the campaign and a call to action. In addition, while not everyone will sign up the first time they learn about your campaign, some may return later to commit to the campaign.

Six tips for an effective text pitch

Follow these tips to make your campaign pitch more effective:

1. Explain why you are asking for money and why crowdfunding is the best, or even only way to raise it.

2. Make sure the campaign feels personal. Give potential backers a way to relate to you and understand your story so they can root for your success.

3. Make backers feel like they are a necessary and meaningful part of the project.

4. Ensure that all spelling, grammar, and formatting is correct.

5. The overview, description, and other details should be clear and concise.

6. Because readers rapidly drop off, the important information should come first.

Crafting a call to action

Both the video and text pitch must include an unambiguous call to action (CTA). It needs to be positive—don't make it seem like you are attempting to force people to back the campaign, or are trying to put a big guilt trip on them. Backers should feel convinced that by becoming part of your wonderful project, they will be helping to do some good in the world, or are helping to bring something great to fruition. Emphasizing the benefits of your project and the good it will achieve contributes to a sense of community, and will encourage people to rally around the campaign.

Earlier, I stressed the importance of adding a personal touch to your campaign assets, such as the video and text pitch. While you want to keep it personal, do not make it seem like the campaign is driven by ego or selfish goals. If potential backers feel they need to contribute or else you will never get to do something that *you* want to do, the campaign will come across as very self-serving, and backers will feel distanced from the outcome of the campaign.

Finally, your call to action must encourage people to make a pledge. You need to assertively, but not aggressively, ask for money to make your campaign a success. Potential backers must believe you need the money and it is going to be used wisely if they decide to get involved.

The wording of the call to action will vary from project to project, but it doesn't have to be elaborate. Here's a sample CTA for a crowdfunding campaign for a film:

> *We appreciate you taking the time to let us tell you about our film. We're excited to get started with production, and we can't wait to share this story with the world! We hope you will join us on our journey and become part of this project! Thank you for backing it today!*

Setting up tiered rewards

Crowdfunding sites typically require campaigns to include a reward system. Rewards are specific objects or benefits the campaign organizer gives backers in exchange for their contributions.

The design of the rewards is hugely important. This may seem surprising to people new to crowdfunding, but there's a reason: In many cases, backers do not actually care about the specific rewards. Rather, they are psychologically inclined to support a campaign in which they receive a reward that has a perceived value close to the actual value of the contribution.

This places creators in a bind. If the goal of the campaign is to raise money to complete a project, organizers can't blow the entire budget on rewards or there will be nothing left for other crucial parts of the campaign. It is therefore essential to minimize the costs of these rewards while still making backers feel appreciated. In the case of entrepreneurial, product-based campaigns, the rewards system, and really the campaign itself, is essentially just a presale system for the product. In all other cases, creators will benefit tremendously from finding ways to provide benefits to backers without incurring significant overhead costs.

The design of the reward structure also determines what type of campaign backer you are seeking. In fact, the first few times I designed rewards for crowdfunding campaigns led to some soul-searching. Was I running campaigns to build relationships with backers, or was it to collect money?

If rewards start at contributions of $1,000, it's very clear to people browsing your campaign that you are seeking fewer backers who are willing to provide a greater commitment. If rewards start at $1, you probably value establishing a relationship with backers. A single backer may not be making a big contribution. In the future, though, he or she could provide more significant financial support once the product is available or support the project in other useful ways, such as by promoting it to their friends.

Unless you are raising money for charity or running a cause-based campaign, you should never view contributions as "donations." Further, avoid words that people associate with charitable contributions, such as "donate" or "charity." Such language implies that there is no specific gain or return for backers. For certain types of crowdfunding projects, such as entrepreneurial or product-based endeavors, people will be skittish if they are portrayed as charitable givers.

How much will people be willing to give? It really depends on the project, the audience, and the rewards. Other factors can come into play, too. Kickstarter notes its most popular pledge level is $25, the most popular pledge day is Wednesday, and backers most often make pledges in the early afternoon.

Visualize Somerville, one of the crowdfunding projects mentioned in the introduction, attracted 96 backers in May of 2016 to support a collective art installation in Somerville, Massachusetts. One of the most popular tiers was $35, which included a free T-shirt and the backer's name projected on the wall when the event took place. At the $100 tier, five backers received one-month memberships at an indoor rock-climbing gym. Overall, backers contributed more than $4,000, making the installation a huge success!

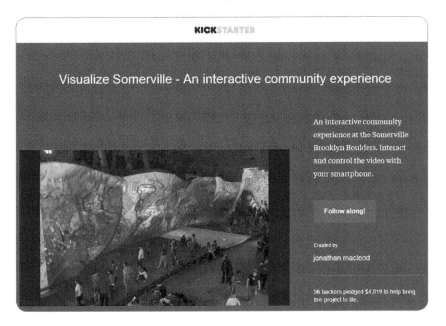

Sample rewards, from $1 to over $100

Reward levels will vary depending on the specific needs and outcomes of a campaign. Regardless of the type of campaign you are running, similar principles apply. In the sample breakdown given below, while the rewards are for a film production, the general ideas and strategies can be applied to almost any kind of crowdfunding project.

→ $1: An official thank-you on the website and in the film credits.

A $1 pledge does very little to help a campaign achieve its goals. In fact, depending on the crowdfunding site and other financial details, base fees for collecting an individual contribution may be so high that a $1 contribution will yield almost no money that can be spent on other elements of the campaign. Nonetheless, I highly recommend allowing people to get involved with a campaign at the $1 level.

In purely financial terms, a $1 tier may seem like a waste of your time, resources, and money. However, a $1 contribution can be tremendously useful in terms of engagement, involvement, and friendship. It allows for people with limited financial resources to be part of your project with what is effectively a gesture of support.

For my own campaigns, I truly value the participation of our $1 contributors. We follow up and thank them the same way that we thank people committing at higher levels. We also communicate with them the same way during and after the campaign, and we try to include final project acknowledgements for these contributors. In fact, for films, one of the most popular rewards for contributors is a "thank you" credit in the film itself, which also ends up on the Internet Movie Database (IMDb). For music projects, the thank you may appear in the liner notes. For brick and mortar stores or restaurants that run a crowdfunding campaign, this could be an acknowledgement appearing on a plaque on the wall.

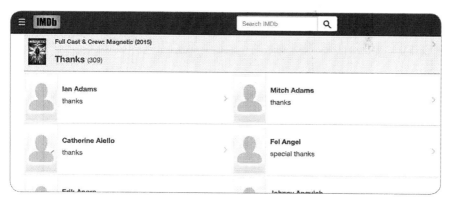

Later, we will discuss reward fulfillment in more detail. But there is a marketing angle related to thank-you rewards while the campaign is still running: Backers often share social media posts that thank them by name, or will share with their friends the fact that their names appear in a thank-you credit on a website. This may help attract other backers from their respective social circles.

→ **$5: An official thank-you on the website and in the film credits, and a postcard from the set signed by members of the film's cast and crew.**

In our campaigns, we have tried to find ways to include a personalized physical object as a low-tier reward. Postcards are excellent rewards for this purpose. They are relatively cheap to make and distribute (about $1 per card), and recipients like getting them—these days, getting personal mail is unusual! Cast and crew sign the cards and write a personal message or a mysterious quote from the film. Everything, including the address, is written by hand, to give a fuller sense of connection between backers and the creative team.

→ **$10: A digital download of the original film score, an official thank-you, and a signed postcard.**

→ **$20: A digital download copy of the film and digital download of the original film score, an official thank-you, and a signed postcard.**

As the pledge amount goes up, the rewards increase. However, we avoid providing costly physical rewards until a relatively high tier. The goal is to maximize connection with the backers and value of their experience while minimizing the corresponding overhead. So, for the $10 and $20 tiers, we offer the digital download of the score and film, as opposed to physical copies.

In addition, we have found that the $20 level is a good place to provide the actual outcome of the project—in this case, a digital download of the film. Many backers will want to back projects to get access to the actual creation, but are financially limited.

→ **$30: A limited-edition, signed DVD of the film as well as a CD of the original film score, a digital download copy of the film and digital download of the original film score, an official thank-you, and a signed postcard.**

Some backers want to receive a physical copy of the project outcome. For campaign organizers, this can be tricky because it immediately adds a significant overhead expense to the project—not only does the object have to be produced, but it also needs to be shipped.

Another consideration: Reward tiers should always be structured so that backers are not receiving any less value than future customers will receive. I have witnessed terrible backlash against campaign organizers who provided only DVDs or CDs as rewards at a $25 backer tier and then imme-diately went on to make copies available to the general public for just $10. It is really important that backers do not feel cheated. So, while you may be tempted to use an inflated reward system similar to charity rewards (such as a public broadcasting fundraiser) remember that the objects offered in charity campaigns are exclusive to the campaign, and are typically never available to the public.

A strategy we have used to get around this issue is to produce a signed and limited "special edition" DVD of our films that only goes to backers. That way, when the retail edition is available, it will be different and hopefully less enticing.

It is also important to give backers early access to content. So, if they receive a copy of the film several months before others, they will feel like that pro-vides some additional value to their experience.

If you do send out a physical object to backers pledging at higher tier levels, pay attention to budget issues! In our film crowdfunding campaign, the $20 tier actually generated more money than the $30 tier after DVD and CD production and shipping costs were factored in.

Finally, all remaining tiers are upsells of the physical product or special experiences and forms of recognition. The reward strategy will now be focused on designing rewards that cost as little as possible to create and deliver but attract higher contributions.

→ **$40: A hand-made cassette "mix tape" copy of the score, a signed DVD of the film as well as a CD of the original film score, a digital download copy of the film and digital download of the original film score, an official thank-you, and a signed postcard.**
For one of our films, *Magnetic*, we had a reward tier that included a cassette copy of the soundtrack, presented in a physical form similar to the cassettes that played a significant role in the film itself. While cassettes are unlikely

to be an appropriate tie-in for most projects, there may be other objects associated with your campaign that can excite and connect backers.

→ **$50: A VIP ticket to a special screening of the film or early streaming access with Q&A for non-local backers (add $10 for a second ticket), a "mix tape" of the score, a signed DVD of the film as well as a CD of the original film score, a digital download copy of the film and digital download of the original film score, an official thank-you, and a signed postcard.**

Starting at the $50 level, we provide rewards that grant access to the creative team and offer exclusive events associated with the film. People pledging at this level are inherently enthusiastic and supportive and want to enjoy the outcome because they are proud to be associated with the campaign.

The early access is also useful in a creative sense. We have often recut or even reshot elements of films after the early presentation to higher-tier backers based on their comments or questions about the film.

Organizing and executing these kinds of screenings has required a big logistical effort, sometimes at a significant cost. It is important to carefully consider whether something like this is a good fit for your project. It may not be appropriate or feasible for all types of projects.

Higher-level rewards

At $60, we might add a signed poster to the reward package. At $75, a T-shirt or tote could be sent to backers. Again, a careful consideration of the costs involved with producing and shipping these rewards is important.

While most backers will fall into the aforementioned tiers, most our campaign income often comes from fewer contributions made at higher tiers. For contributions ranging from $100 to several thousands of dollars, we try to look at how to create personalized experiences. The possibilities for personalization are endless, but here are a few examples from our film-based campaigns:

➤ The cast and crew will record a one-take lip sync video to the song of your choosing.

➤ Your art appears in our film.

➤ Your name is mentioned as an off-screen character in our film (with IMDb credit).

➤ You make an on-screen cameo in our film (with IMDb credit).

➤ You receive a prop from the film.

➤ You receive the film slate used in production of the film.

➤ You receive an individual cast member or crew member's signed script with his or her notes included.

➤ A coffee date with the producers or a short consultation on a project.

➤ We will do something that uses some other creative skill that we have, such as record a song about you or paint a portrait of you.

➤ Receive an associate or executive producer credit (submitted to IMDb).

➤ We will produce a short film for you.

Tier level vs. backer support

When it comes to popularity of different tiers, each campaign is unique—it really depends on the nature of the project, the backer community, and the reward tiers. Here's how a typical campaign for one of my creative projects breaks down:

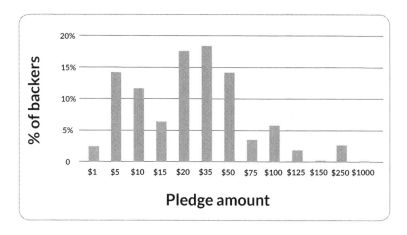

Nine best practices for structuring rewards

1. Be creative and exude the spirit, excitement, and enthusiasm of your campaign in your reward descriptions.

2. Use reward levels to convey the types of relationships you would like to have with backers. Are they personal or transactional? Are they long term or short term?

3. Many sites allow you to name reward tiers. Have fun with the names!

4. Spell out the full reward at each tier rather than saying "plus all the earlier rewards" or "plus all $50 rewards." This makes it much easier for backers to understand what they are getting.

5. Make sure the values of the rewards fit the contribution.

6. Exclusive rewards are ideal. Avoid rewards that are identical to products that will be available to the public unless the cost to the public will be significantly higher.

7. Offer unique access and special experiences for backers even if they otherwise have no association with the project. Often, backers just like to get access to the team members!

8. Most crowdfunding sites allow you to include a delivery date for rewards. Consider making that date later, as you are very likely to run into unexpected delays. Backers will be pleased to receive their rewards early, but may be anxious or unhappy if they turn up late.

9. Overhead costs, including time and effort, need to be realistically estimated for each reward. Crowdfunding sites often allow limits for specific reward tiers. While you may like to receive money from hundreds of backers for a certain reward tier, it may not be feasible to prepare them in a reasonable timeframe if it involves painting portraits of each one.

CHAPTER 4

Running the campaign

By now it should be clear that planning a crowdfunding campaign is hard work, from setting up a budget to designing reward tiers. However, the bulk of focused time you will spend on a campaign will happen after the launch, when the campaign is running. We have already discussed finding backers via social circles, communities, and the media. Keeping these backers engaged will be a big part of your campaign, but there are other important tasks that can't be ignored.

How to get people excited about your campaign

You've got a great campaign planned. Your video is compelling, your text is exciting, and your rewards are irresistible. Now, how do you get people to check out your campaign and get involved?

Connecting with backers

As outlined in Chapter 2, the initial backers for your first campaign will consist of friends, family, and existing fans. You have already planned your campaign budget based on projected pledges from these groups. Ideally, some will eagerly commit to your campaign as soon as it launches.

This group can be regarded as your seed investors. They will help you sow initial momentum and will do a first round of promotions by demonstrating early support. However, their contributions will generally wrap up early in the campaign. So how do you reach the rest?

Social media and email outreach

Many campaign organizers turn to existing broadcast platforms such as social media feeds and email lists to distribute campaign announcements. However, if the updates and marketing messages become a firehose, it can turn off backers.

For email, it may be best to send just one or two emails to your fans over the full course of the campaign. Because you are only sending a few messages, each one should be carefully structured to excite them and encourage them to take action.

Social media is trickier. There are countless platforms, each with its own best practices. For Facebook and Twitter, followers may see only a small percentage of the messages you post. This may require regularly repeating content so more people get the message.

I usually post once or twice per day and ensure that every post includes some small piece of new information or content. Social media works best when there is engagement, so asking questions, taking polls, or sparking topical discussions can be very effective.

Social media best practices

➤ Intersperse campaign posts with "normal" posts to keep your overall engagement as high as possible. Social media platforms rely on the popularity of your last post to determine how many people will receive the posts that follow.

➤ Make posts personal and humorous rather than informational and dry. Always use funny anecdotes, compelling photos, and other media to connect with people.

Michael J. Epstein
October 7, 2013 · 🌐

You may have noticed me complaining about sci-fi movies. We're giving a go at making something interesting for about $10,000, which is 1/10,000th the cost of Gravity, 1/11,500th the cost of Elysium, and 1/19,000th the cost of Pacific Rim. I promise we will make something at least 1/10,000th as good as all three. A bargain really.

MAGNETIC - A psychological sci-fi feature film
KICKSTARTER.COM

➤ Provide a way for supporters and collaborators to share posts and content to boost the messages.

➤ Use topical hashtags and keywords to expand the reach beyond your immediate connections.

➤ Look for Facebook pages, Twitter lists, and other social media groups that might be interested in your project and post information to them. Be sure to follow the posting rules for these groups.

For more information on how to effectively engage with other people on social media, check out some of the other titles in the In 30 Minutes series, such as *Twitter In 30 Minutes* and *LinkedIn In 30 Minutes*. More information can be found at in30minutes.com.

Personal appeals

After the campaign starts, you may want to selectively reach out to friends, family, and other fans to personally ask them if they would consider supporting your campaign. If done correctly, it can be very effective—most people will be supportive. As with all communications regarding your campaign, be sure to write about it using positive or uplifting language rather than language that evokes guilt or other negative emotions. Your campaign is all about the great things that will happen if it's successful. Inspire those who care about your happiness and success, and make it clear that you want to bring them along on your journey. Here's an example of an appeal from a crowdfunded donation campaign for people with intellectual and developmental disabilities:

> *Please know that you would not be sending money to me, but to people in need of a lifetime of support. If you can spare anything, I'd be greatly appreciative. No donation is too small. If you want to donate $1, that'd be great! If you can skip your next Starbuck's coffee and donate, that would be even better! The individual recipients of the program and their families will be just as appreciative as well.*
>
> *If you'd like to donate, please look at the link below (and make sure it's a link to my donation page) and consider donating any amount that you'd like.*

Conversely, never demand that any of your friends, family, or fans support your campaign. There should be no repercussions to anyone for not giving. People should contribute because they want to be a part of your campaign. When someone does contribute, you should always appreciate his or her support.

Spreading the word: a team effort

Many campaigns involve more than a single organizer or creator. While it is useful to have most of your communication come from a spokesperson, everyone involved with your campaign can and should be sharing information on their social media streams, making personal pleas to friends and family, and publicly demonstrating their own enthusiasm for the project. Try to create content that your team members can easily share. In fact, you may want to do feature profiles about all team members so they feel recognized and their connections will see how essential they are to the project.

Finding niche communities

One of the most successful strategies in crowdfunding (and marketing in general) is identifying not only a demographic with a general interest in your project, but also those niche audiences that may have a deep-seated interest. Certain special interest or fandom groups want to support projects that are tied closely with their members' interests. In many cases, they feel dutifully bound to do so. Try to identify elements in your project or cause that may resonate with these groups. Engaging a niche group may also help attract press attention.

For several years, I have played in a band with songs inspired by the cult British television series *The Prisoner* (trust me, it's a great show!). We follow two important principles:

1. Nothing we do should alienate an audience unfamiliar with the series.
2. Those who are familiar with the series should find something to connect with.

As a result of cultivating this niche audience, we have been extensively supported by fans of the series and even invited to play conventions and fandom events associated with *The Prisoner*.

This has worked well for us not only because there is a strong, established fandom, but also because it is an obscure enough niche that we are unique. A crowdfunding campaign targeting a niche audience will often receive enthusiastic support because there is a strong desire for more associated content, even if it is just tangentially related and made by fans.

When you seek possible niche communities, look for novelty and depth of enthusiasm. Besides film and television tie-ins, other examples of crowdfunding campaigns targeting a niche audience might include manufacturing a part for a specific kind of vintage bicycle or a documentary about a once-popular video game from the 1990s. However, the more commonplace the product or broad the target audience, the harder it will be to take advantage of niche communities.

Attracting press interest

An entire book could be written on strategies for attracting and communicating with newspapers, broadcasters, magazines, and specialist online publications, but there are some essentials. The most important things to remember when reaching out to the press:

1. Media outlets need stories to fill space or take up time.

2. Reporters, editors, and hosts are being pitched far too many stories for the space they have available.

While there are no guaranteed ways to get press coverage, a good starting point is to identify the outlets for which your story is a perfect fit. You hopefully believe that your campaign is brilliant and everyone should care about it, but reporters at major newspapers or producers at TV stations are extremely unlikely to feel the same way.

Niche and local media are a different story. While many larger outlets have a blanket ban on crowdfunding campaigns, your local town newspaper may consider a feature on your campaign, especially if there is a strong local angle.

Another attention-getting angle involves creating a wildly successful campaign. Publications can't resist news of a small-scale campaign raising hundreds of thousands of even millions of dollars. While this type of coverage usually comes after the campaign is over, it can help spread interest in the product, project, or cause to a much wider audience. One such campaign was profiled on the AgFunderNews website:

Crowdfunding campaign raised $2M in 24 hours for Honey on Tap

🕐 FEBRUARY 23, 2015   👤 ROB LECLERC

Move over drones and Oculus Rift. There's a new technology disrupting … the beekeeping industry. Flow Hive, with its patented beehive design, has raised $2M on the crowdfunding site Indiegogo since its campaign launched less than 24 hours ago. Already this eclipsed its goal of $70K, and placed it at #11 of

Best practices for approaching media

Reporters and editors receive scores or even hundreds of press releases per day. Many are from publicists with whom they have personal connections. Thus, it is important for you to find a way for your story to stand out when emailing a journalist you don't know. If you are reaching out to a writer whose work you regularly read, briefly introduce yourself and state why your story fits in with previous topics he or she has covered in the past.

Notice how I keep using the word "story"? Good writers do more than simply state the facts—they try to tell stories. So, when you are pitching the media, make sure the pitch contains a narrative. For instance, it is much more interesting to learn about what gave you the idea for your campaign than simply listing the bare-bones facts about the campaign.

When I send out press releases, I use prose that can be quickly copied and pasted into an article. Lots of publications don't have the resources to write original articles for everything they want to cover, so you are doing them a favor by making it easy for writers and editors to repurpose a press release. Of course, this is a big benefit for your campaign, as you will have the opportunity to present your story exactly as you want audiences to see it.

That said, it is unlikely that broadcasting press releases will yield much coverage. This is where outside help can be useful—a good publicist will be able to evaluate your story, and then decide which one of his or her media connections to personally reach out to. They will have a much higher success rate because of personal knowledge and their relationships with writers and editors.

Hiring a publicist can easily cost thousands of dollars (in fact, I would be wary of trusting a publicist who charges very little). If the costs are prohibitive or inappropriate for your campaign, you can certainly do it yourself. Just be sure to craft an exciting and novel story. As with niche communities, the more narrowly specific and novel the elements of your story are, the easier it will be to create narratives around them.

For example, one campaign that received a lot of press coverage was *Carver*, a horror film that was co-created by a 13-year-old girl. There is novelty and excitement when a young female creator takes on a project in a field that is both predominantly male and generally requires actors and other participants to be older. The press loved it, and the news of the campaign was widely reported online and in print. A horror film made by a 40-year-old guy would not have been able to use gender or age as a storytelling point when pitching the media.

Remember, many outlets have long lead times on stories, so reach out well in advance of your campaign launch. Some outlets will also want to break "fresh" stories and will prefer to cover your project on launch day. Other writers will become interested in reporting your story only after they see coverage elsewhere, so be sure to leverage existing articles about your campaign to pitch new outlets.

The art of communicating with backers

As a campaign organizer, you are going to receive lots of questions from potential backers. Answer them kindly and promptly, even if the questions have already been answered in your campaign materials.

There is an associated benefit of getting questions and comments: They serve as valuable feedback that can point to missing or unclear information in your campaign materials. Based on this feedback, you may be able to revise your campaign. Each crowdfunding website has its own policy about revisions and modifications after a campaign has launched, but there are generally ways to add, modify, or clarify information. Many sites also allow organizers to add new reward levels.

Besides communicating with potential backers, you will want to thank people after they contribute. For all of the campaigns I have worked on, the team sends thank you videos to backers immediately after they make commitments. The videos are not only fun and personal, but they also have often led to backers increasing pledge amounts.

As you can imagine, individualized videos take time to record, upload, tag, and email. Time is as precious a resource as any. However, showing a commitment to your backers gives them a greater sense of involvement. The time spent on cultivating relationships with backers is an investment that can be very worthwhile. Moreover, it doesn't have to be a video: Even just a short, personal message is very useful for making backers feel appreciated.

Keeping the momentum going

Campaigns tend to follow a pattern that looks something like this:

➤ **Successful launch.** The planning and preparations have paid off. Early backers pledge their support and share the news with their friends.

➤ **Mid-campaign lull.** Funding growth slows, and there are not as many new backers as you had hoped. The longer the lull, the more likely feelings of panic are to seep in.

➤ **Strong ending.** People are really excited for the campaign. More people join up, and you are finally able to reach your funding goal.

What happens when the pledges slow, or come to a complete halt? I have seen many campaign creators get discouraged during the second week of a 30-day campaign because activity has slowed to a trickle. This is not terribly unusual, but if it does happen, be sure to increase your promotional efforts, and maybe even look at your full campaign plan to see if there is a particularly exciting update you can move up in your schedule to rekindle excitement about the project.

The graph below shows the path to funding for the first three film campaigns I was involved with:

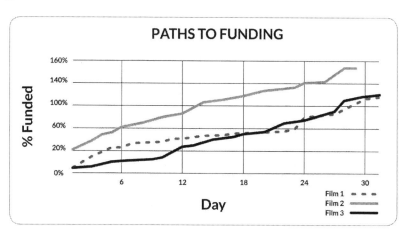

The strategies for each campaign were slightly different.

➤ Film #1: For the first campaign, we did a large push early. We then ran out of steam and had no real plan for the middle section in which growth was stagnant.

➤ Film #2: For the second campaign, we were better at spacing contributions. However, we set the goal too low, so we rapidly exceeded the goal and then had to think about how to convince people to continue contributing using stretch goals.

➤ Film #3: For the third campaign, we intentionally asked people to space their contributions over a longer period of time, rather than all at once. This helped keep growth and momentum throughout the campaign.

As you get better at planning and executing campaigns, you will find it easier to coordinate the release of updates and information to keep pledges rolling in. You will also start to find it easier to choose an appropriate goal for your campaign. Beginners are more likely to do a great job of finding that initial 20-30% of funding, but get a little stuck on getting the word out after that. You will need to find a way to grow your story each day to continue to ramp up the excitement for your campaign.

Tell your story daily

During the campaign, you will need to find a middle ground between sending your backers too many updates via the crowdfunding platform and not providing enough information. Backers who have committed to a project are probably happy to see just a few updates over the course of the campaign. I often aim to send out backer updates about once per week, with a few additional updates right near the end of the campaign to take advantage of the excitement during the final push.

While committed backers only require infrequent communication, potential backers may not act until they have connected with your campaign several times. As discussed in the social media section, more frequent updates are warranted for this group—ideally, daily communications with new bits of content or information. For example, the film campaigns I've worked on typically release one actor profile per day during the course of the campaign.

For optimal visibility, it's useful to share different types of content, including audio, video, photos, and text. This will require significant advance planning, as most of this content needs to be prepared before the campaign is launched. There may also be new content, such as press coverage, that cannot be planned in advance, but will be inserted into your posting schedule as it becomes available.

Depending on the system you are using to run your campaign, you may prefer to post these updates to your website or blog rather than on the campaign page. For instance, I often post actor profiles to my personal blog and then link them in the campaign text as they are released rather than just posting them as updates to the campaign page itself. This prevents current backers from receiving too many email notifications of additional information about the project, but allows the posting of new blog links to social media each day.

Why campaigns fail: 10 pitfalls to avoid

Historically, about two-thirds of crowdfunding campaigns fail. While the crowdfunding best practices in this book should help you beat the odds, it's worth keeping in mind why campaigns may stumble and fail. Here are ten reasons:

1. **No pre-planning:** Creators believe their ideas are so good that they can simply throw them up on crowdfunding websites and the money will roll right in. Simply put, it does not matter how good your idea is—crowdfunding requires a lot of hard work.

2. **Poor visual assets:** The photos, videos, and other visuals used to support campaigns require excitement and professionalism to spark the imaginations of potential backers. Don't depend on your smartphone's camera!

3. **Too long, too wordy, too obtuse:** Backers don't want to know every single detail about your plans. They expect to hear a clear, concise, compelling pitch. Keep it simple. Keep it brief.

4. **Not enough details:** While your ideas must be clear, you also have to include enough information to let backers know that your proposal is realistic.

5. **Unrealistically high budget:** Although a few campaigns end up hitting it big, your campaign will never raise millions of dollars. In fact, unrealistic targets can lead to fewer contributions—prospective backers will simply skip pledging.

6. **Unrealistically low budget:** You are going to build a rocket ship to launch into orbit and your campaign is seeking $250. Potential backers will not believe you can do it.

7. **No novelty:** Your project needs to spark the imagination of backers, or get them really interested in supporting you. If your idea is too similar to existing products, backers will choose someone with bigger dreams.

8. **Early burnout:** After a week has passed and you are still below your target, it's so easy to give up. For crowdfunding campaigns, slow and steady wins the race. You will need sustained energy to see you through to the end.

9. **Bad rewards:** If your rewards are boring or don't live up to their value tiers, your campaign is more likely to be passed over by potential backers.

10. **The partial-funding trap:** This really comes back to your budget. If you truly need a certain amount of money to complete a project, yet you are choosing a partial-funding platform, how can you be trusted to complete it if the campaign comes in below the target?

Sample campaign timeline

Now that you know what works and you know what does not work when it comes to operating your crowdfunding campaign, it is time to make plans and launch. Here is a quick outline of a possible timeline for a generic campaign, from start to finish. The schedule will vary depending on many things, including existing support and the type of press and media you hope to attract, but it should give you a rough idea of how to get started.

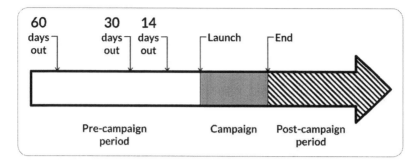

> ➤ **60 days before launch:** Begin creating your content such as campaign video and text for the website. If applicable, start to chart out the reward tiers (as described in Chapter 3).

> ➤ **30 days before launch:** Send campaign materials to trusted friends to get feedback, and make modifications based on their suggestions. Ask if they are willing to get involved once the campaign launches.

> ➤ **At least 14 days before launch:** Reach out to media outlets and relate your story. Continue this process throughout the campaign as notable coverage occurs or new information surfaces (see Chapter 4).

> ➤ **Launch Day:** Reach out to friends who have promised to get involved. Begin social media, email, and other direct campaigns to potential backers (Chapter 4).

> ➤ **During the campaign:** Thank backers as they commit. Consider providing no-cost rewards to backers (on many crowdfunding platforms backers can withdraw contributions, so it's a good idea to keep them engaged). For potential backers, make daily social media updates and weekly campaign updates (Chapter 4).

> ➤ **Campaign completion:** Thank backers (again) and collect information to distribute rewards.

> ➤ **Post-campaign updates:** Let backers know the project is still moving forward. Give monthly/bimonthly updates to backers until the project is complete and rewards are fulfilled (Chapter 5).

CHAPTER 5

After the campaign

Breathe a sigh of relief! The campaign has ended and you have reached your funding goal. It's time to collect your money and get started on your project.

Not so fast! There are a few other things you need to do, even after the money has been transferred to your bank account. As you move forward, you must continue to acknowledge your backers and provide them with updates. For many crowdfunding campaigns, especially those associated with a creative or entrepreneurial projects, you will need to provide rewards.

Post-funding activities

Immediately after a campaign ends, creators typically send out group or individual thank-you messages. It's important to let backers know their support is really appreciated—because of their contributions, the campaign was a success, and the plan can proceed now that funds are ready. This initial post-funding communication does not need to be elaborate, but it should be heartfelt and continue to make backers feel connected to the project.

Crowdfunding systems typically provide post-funding surveys designed to collect the necessary information for distributing rewards and staying in touch with backers. Most backers will expect to receive a survey from you soon after funding is confirmed.

A word of warning: If you collect mailing addresses immediately, be sure to check in with backers when rewards are ready to be mailed out. The longer the gap between the campaign closing and the rewards being sent out, the more likely people will have changed addresses.

Also, keep in mind that many backers will not respond to emails or messages on crowdfunding sites. You may need to spend some time following up to contact them for additional information. Be proactive and do not just assume they are ignoring messages and are responsible for omissions.

Staying in touch with backers

Backers place tremendous trust on creators to follow through with whatever they have promised during the campaign. Backers will want to hear monthly or bimonthly updates of progress. Some creators provide backer-only updates, giving exclusive access to news about the project. Others choose to make all updates available to the general public. Either of these strategies, or a mix of the two, can be effectively utilized to engage backers and even prospective customers or fans who were not backers during the campaign.

As noted earlier, a high percentage of successfully funded campaigns do not ultimately complete their proposed projects or send the promised rewards. For this reason, backers will become nervous in the absence of updates. They will appreciate any evidence of progress toward completion, and will also want to receive promised rewards as they become available.

What if the progress is not good? No one likes to deliver bad news, and campaign organizers are understandably reluctant to reveal problems or delays. However, backers prefer honest communication from organizers, even if it's negative. Most of the time, they are forgiving ... as long as there is a plan for completion and delivery of rewards.

Fulfilling rewards

Tracking and fulfilling rewards is a surprisingly complex and challenging part of a crowdfunding campaign. As explained in Chapter 2, campaigns involving creative or entrepreneurial projects will involve many different types of rewards with varying combinations given at the different tiers.

Try to fulfill rewards as soon as possible. People are counting on you to fulfill rewards on a timely basis, and procrastination on your part can lead to frustration. An exception involves backers who are supposed to receive multiple rewards, but only part of the shipment is ready to go. Because postage costs tend to make up a significant portion of campaign overhead, it's acceptable to wait until everything is ready (but be sure to communicate the situation to affected backers). If your backers are local, it may help to hand-deliver portions of their rewards if it's convenient. Doing so will potentially cut a lot of the project's shipping overhead.

There are several ways to track rewards for individual backers. I usually create a spreadsheet in Google Sheets or Microsoft Excel with a row for each backer and a column for each reward. I then immediately mark which rewards each backer should receive and mark them as completed as they are fulfilled. This structure is useful because some of the rewards are generally fulfilled during the campaign or immediately after, whereas others will not be fulfilled until a year or more after the campaign initially ran.

A ◂ ▸ D ◂ ▸ I			J	K	L	M	N
Backer #	Pledge	Postcard	DVD	Shirt Size	Added to credits	NOTES	Lip Sync
29	$100.00	YES	YES	Unisex small-GA\	x		Eagles/Hotel California
28	$25.00	YES	N/A	N/A			N/A
27	$50.00	YES	YES	N/A	x		N/A
26	$50.00	YES	YES	N/A			N/A
25	$100.00	YES	YES	mailed shirt		MAILED SHIRT	Outsider - Hero (ft. LMN
24	$35.00	YES	YES	N/A			N/A
23	$20.00	YES	N/A	N/A			N/A
22	$35.00	YES	YES	N/A			N/A
21	$35.00	YES	YES	N/A			N/A
20	$10.00	YES	N/A	N/A	x		N/A
19	$250.00	YES	YES	Womens 2XL	x	MAILED EVERY	N/A
18	$20.00	YES	N/A	N/A			N/A
17	$100.00	YES	YES	womens small			Katrina & The Waves -
16	$50.00	YES	YES	N/A	x		N/A
15	$10.00	YES	N/A	N/A	x		N/A

Expect to receive frequent questions from anxious backers about the status of the project and their rewards. Some people will get nervous even if you have specified a delivery date well into the future, or have already provided updates via email or an online post. As with all communications with backers, be polite and maintain a positive attitude.

If you are late on delivery, don't fret too much. Almost 75% of the campaigns I have backed have delivered rewards late. Just be sure to communicate the state of progress and assure backers that late rewards will eventually be delivered. Generally, this is well tolerated.

There are exceptions for physical items from entrepreneurial campaigns—backers may feel more like they are buying a product than supporting a dream, and will expect on-time delivery. Nonetheless, nearly all manufacturing campaigns I have backed have run into delays, so experienced crowdfunding backers will know to expect as much.

CONCLUSION

In 30 minutes, we have looked at the types of projects suitable for crowd-funding, examined the costs and benefits of running campaigns, and dug into campaign development and execution. You can put your newfound knowledge to use right away to plan a crowdfunding campaign to support your dream project or cause!

Start by evaluating whether an all-or-nothing model might work best, or whether you prefer partial-funding options. Then, devise a budget based on anticipated project expenditures, reward costs, and other overhead. Prime the pump by reaching out to friends, family, and existing fans who might support your campaign. For other people who might be interested in supporting your campaign, build campaign assets such as text, images, and videos that are compelling and exciting. Once the campaign starts, get your early fans to commit and encourage other prospective backers to get on board. Feed your audience updates and other information about the campaign and the project itself—and be prepared to distribute rewards to backers.

I hope you have had as much fun reading this guide as I had writing it. I truly have enjoyed sharing my crowdfunding experiences and knowledge. You can follow me on Kickstarter to see the campaigns I create and back or learn more about me at my website, MichaelJEpstein.com. You can also follow me on social media via Facebook or Twitter. The official companion website to this book is located at crowdfunding.in30minutes.com and lists all of these links. I would love to see what you are doing with crowdfunding—so please don't hesitate to drop me a line!

I also have a favor to ask. Could you take a few minutes to post an honest review of *Crowdfunding Basics In 30 Minutes*? Real reader reviews not only let others know what to expect, but they also help to raise the book's profile.

Thanks for reading, and best of luck with your campaign!

Michael J. Epstein

Index

Notes

Introduction to Google Drive & Docs In 30 Minutes

The following bonus chapter is the introduction to Google Drive & Docs In 30 Minutes (2nd Edition). To download the ebook or purchase the paperback, visit the book's official website, googledrive.in30minutes.com.

Why you need to use Google's free office suite

Thanks for picking up a copy of *Google Drive & Docs In 30 Minutes,* 2nd Edition. I wrote this unofficial user guide to help people get up to speed with Google's remarkable (and free) online office suite that includes file storage (Google Drive), a word processor (Google Docs), a spreadsheet program (Google Sheets), and a presentation tool (Google Slides).

How do people use these applications? There are many possible uses. Consider these examples:

> ➤ **A harried product manager needs to work on an important proposal over the weekend.** In the past, she would have dug around in her purse to look for an old USB drive she uses for transferring files. Or, she might have emailed herself an attachment to open at home. Not anymore. Now she saves the Word document and an Excel spreadsheet to Google Drive at the office. Later that evening, on her home PC, she opens her Google Drive folder to access and edit the files. All of her saves are updated to Google Drive. When she returns to work the following Monday, the updated data can be viewed at her workstation.

> ➤ **The organizer of a family reunion wants to survey 34 cousins** about attendance, lodging preferences, and potluck dinner preparation (always a challenge—the Nebraska branch of the family won't eat corn or Garbanzo beans). He emails everyone a link to an online form he created using Google Forms. Relatives open the form on their browsers, and submit their answers. The answers are automatically transferred to Sheets, where the organizer can see the responses and tally the results.

> ➤ A small business consultant is helping the owner of Slappy's Canadian Diner (*"We Put The Canadian Back In Bacon"*) **prepare a slideshow for potential franchisees in Ohio**. The consultant and Slappy collaborate using Google Slides, which lets them remotely access the deck and add text, images, and other elements. The consultant shares a link to the slideshow with her consulting partner, so he can periodically review it on the Google Slides app on his phone and check for problems. Later,

Slappy meets his potential franchise operators at a hotel in Cleveland, and uses Google Slides on his iPad to pitch his business.

➤ **An elementary school faculty uses Docs to collaborate on lesson plans.** Each teacher accesses the same document from home or the classroom. Updates are instantly reflected, even when two teachers are simultaneously accessing the same document. Their principal (known as "Skinner" behind his back) is impressed by how quickly the faculty completes the plans, and how well the curriculums are integrated.

➤ At the same school, the 5th-grade teachers **ask their students to submit homework using Docs**. The teachers add corrections and notes, which the students can access at home using a Web browser. It's much more efficient than emailing attachments, and the students don't need to bug their parents to purchase Microsoft Office.

Many people are introduced to Google's online office suite through Docs, the incredibly popular online word processor. Others are attracted by the free storage and syncing features of Google Drive. Microsoft Office, which includes Word, Excel, PowerPoint, and OneDrive, can cost hundreds of dollars. While Drive is not as sophisticated as Microsoft Office, it handles basic documents and spreadsheets very well. Google Drive also offers a slew of powerful online features, including:

➤ The ability to review the history of a specific document, and revert to an earlier version.

➤ Simple Web forms and online surveys which can be produced without programming skills or website hosting arrangements.

➤ Collaboration features that let users work on the same document in real time.

➤ Offline file storage that can be synced to multiple computers.

➤ Automatic notification of the release date of Brad Pitt's next movie.

I'm just kidding about the last item. But Google Drive, Docs, Sheets, Forms, and Slides really can do those other things, and without the help of your company's IT department or the pimply teenager from down the street. These features are built right into the software, and are ready to use as soon as you've signed up.

Even though the myriad features of Google's office suite may seem overwhelming, this guide makes it easy to get started. *Google Drive & Docs In 30 Minutes* is written in plain English, with lots of step-by-step instructions, screenshots and tips. More resources are available on the companion website to this book, *googledrive.in30minutes.com*. You'll get up to speed in no time.

The second edition of *Google Drive & Docs In 30 Minutes* covers recent interface improvements, as well as the expanded capabilities of the Google Drive, Docs, Sheets, and Slides apps for iOS and Android.

We've only got half an hour, so let's get started. If you are using a PC or laptop, please download the Google Chrome browser, which works best with Google Drive, Docs, Slides, and Sheets. Instructions for the Chromebook and the mobile apps are referenced throughout the guide.

> *If you're interested in learning more about this title, or buying the ebook or paperback, visit the official website located at googledrive.in30minutes.com.*

Introduction to LinkedIn In 30 Minutes

The following bonus chapter is the introduction to LinkedIn In 30 Minutes (2nd Edition), by author Angela Rose. This book is a Foreword INDIES Finalist. To download the ebook or purchase the paperback, visit the book's official website, linkedin.in30minutes.com.

I'm going to let you in on a little secret: I haven't always been on LinkedIn. In fact, I wasn't even aware the professional networking platform existed until 2006.

At the time, I was working as a manager in the creative department of a small marketing company. Our clients were primarily in the mortgage and real estate industries, and they would personalize the postcards and newsletters my team and I had created with their logos and contact information before mailing them to their databases. One day a real estate agent asked us to include the web address (or URL) for his LinkedIn profile.

I was intrigued. While I was not a social media newbie—I posted hilarious, adorable and poignant pictures of my cats on Facebook almost every day—the concept of social network for professional people was different. I checked out the agent's profile, took a quick tour of LinkedIn's features, and left it at that. I had a job I loved. I was going to work there until I died. I didn't need what LinkedIn had to offer.

Then the housing bubble burst, causing property values to plummet and thousands of homeowners to default on their mortgages. No one could buy, no one could sell—and our client base began to contract. As we put raises on hold and closed our offices on Fridays, I had to face an unpleasant reality: It was very possible I'd need to find a new job—or strike out on my own—in the near future.

Suddenly, being on LinkedIn looked like a really good idea. I spent 30 minutes that first Friday setting up a free profile. While I only filled out the basics, I felt better having done something that might help me if the unthinkable happened. About one year later, it did. But by then I had built the foundations of a freelance writing and editing business. I had more than a dozen regular clients, and their assignments were enough, along with some savings, to ensure I'd be able to keep paying my bills (and feeding those cats) as I continued to grow The Quirky Creative.

LinkedIn helped me make it happen. I made a habit of connecting with the decision-makers at every company that used my services. This kept me front of mind, and resulted in referrals and repeat assignments. I asked for—and gave—recommendations, then shared the glowing endorsements with potential clients. This helped me to land more assignments. I added a professional photo, packed my background summary with keywords and personality, and uploaded clips from my growing portfolio of published work.

With every enhancement, my profile received more views. I received more emails from professionals and companies interested in the services I provided. I landed more assignments—and I was able to maintain the lifestyle to which my cats were accustomed (i.e. gourmet kibble, frequent catnip binges and all the toy mice they could shove under the sofa).

In fact, LinkedIn actually led to the book you are reading today. The publisher of In 30 Minutes guides found my profile, liked the contents, and offered me the opportunity to share what I've learned about using this increasingly important social media platform with all of you—no cat photos required!

Not just an online resume

As the above anecdote illustrates, LinkedIn is more than just an online catalog of former employers and responsibilities. It's a tool that can have a significant—and positive—impact on your life, whether you use it to search for a new job, network with other professionals in your industry, establish an online presence or even learn more about potential vendors and service providers (I used it to 'vet' my cats' veterinarian).

Consider the following numbers:

➤ LinkedIn has approximately 400 million members, located in practically every country in the world. Whether you want to connect with a former supervisor, a colleague you met at a conference, the recruiter at your dream company, or even your old high school track coach (go Warriors!), you are likely to find them on LinkedIn.

➤ According to a recent LinkedIn report, the network hosts more than 3 million active job listings. Advertised positions are in dozens of industries ranging from agriculture and construction to finance and healthcare. Whatever your area of expertise, you are likely to find employment opportunities on LinkedIn.

➤ A 2014 Jobvite Social Recruiting Survey found that 93% of recruiters use or plan to use social media platforms to fill jobs. Among these recruiters, 94% use LinkedIn. Whether you are actively searching for a new job or are a passive candidate—defined as interested in opportunities though not active in the job search—joining LinkedIn will make it easier for employers to find you.

How are people leveraging LinkedIn?

While students and recent college grads are the fastest growing demographic on LinkedIn, the social media network has more than 80 million members between the ages of 30 and 49, and more than 100 million who are 50 years of age or older.

How are they using their profiles? Here are just a few examples:

➤ **Matthew is an account rep for a large biopharma company.** A frequent trade show attendee, he uses LinkedIn to learn more about the professionals he plans to network with on his trips ... and later uses LinkedIn to maintain connections afterward. This has helped him land new accounts as well as forge relationships that may prove valuable when it's time to take the next step in his career.

➤ **Samantha is a recent college graduate with a degree in human resources management.** She is currently interviewing for jobs as a payroll administrator, and she uses LinkedIn to learn more about the companies she is visiting as well as the professionals conducting the interviews. Thanks to the keywords in her profile, she has been approached by a number of recruiters for jobs she otherwise wouldn't have heard about.

➤ **John is a freelance graphic designer.** While he hasn't had a regular 9-to-5 job in the last decade, he has used the experience section of his LinkedIn profile to feature several of his current and former contract projects. With dozens of recommendations and hundreds of endorsements, his profile enhances his professional reputation.

➤ **Amanda was laid off in December.** She has been using LinkedIn to search for a new job in the healthcare industry. A registered nurse, she has connected with the hiring managers at several local hospitals using InMail. She is a member of a half-dozen nursing- and healthcare-related groups and regularly participates in discussions to increase her visibility. She has also spent time enhancing her LinkedIn profile with a current, professional photo and keywords to improve her search ranking.

➤ **Robert is a retired fireman.** He's not interested in going back to work full-time, or even part-time for that matter, but he likes to see what former colleagues are doing and stay current on the latest industry news. He uses LinkedIn to connect with other public safety professionals, learn new information about the field, and share his experience and opinions with the members of related discussion groups.

Are you ready to get started?

Whatever your age, profession, or employment status, you are almost certain to benefit from learning to use LinkedIn—and doing so is surprisingly easy. It doesn't matter if you are a complete newbie or a frequent social media consumer, this guide will show you how to navigate the LinkedIn platform, register for a free account, set up your profile step-by-step, connect with other members, join discussion groups and search for jobs—all in the time it would take to watch a dozen YouTube cat videos. We only have 30 minutes, so let's get started!

If you're interested in learning more about this title, or buying the ebook or paperback, visit the official website located at linkedin.in30minutes.com.

Introduction to Genealogy Basics In 30 Minutes

The following bonus chapter is the introduction to the award-winning Genealogy Basics In 30 Minutes, by author Shannon Combs-Bennett. To download the ebook or purchase the paperback, visit the book's official website, genealogy.in30minutes.com.

When I was a child, I liked to listen to my family share family stories. At six years of age, sometimes I would hide away, just out of eyesight, as the adults discussed a memory or a special someone from decades past. The tales were often exciting or funny. Others were serious or sad. The characters— so interesting! And they were all connected to me and my family!

I found out that my maternal grandmother's father was 61 years old when she was born. She said that when my great-grandfather was a child, he could recall holding his mother's hand, watching his older brothers in their Union blues marching off to fight in the Civil War. My imagination ran!

Fast forward a few decades, and my love of family stories has blossomed into a full-fledged career as a professional genealogist. Now, in addition to researching my own family history, I help other people learn more about their families' histories. This book is another way for me to help people learn about their ancestors and become effective stewards of their families' histories.

Why are people interested in family history?

People of all ages and backgrounds are flocking to the field of genealogy in ever-increasing numbers. What's behind the surge? I think the interest has always been there, but in recent years media and technology have changed the dynamics. Consider these factors:

➤ The widespread availability of inexpensive or free software for managing family records.

➤ Easier access to vital records and other data, thanks to online databases, social networks, and email.

➤ Television programs such as *History Detectives* and *Finding Your Roots*, which explain basic research concepts and share interesting genealogy stories involving famous people.

➤ Ever-present ads telling consumers how "easy" it is to trace your family tree.

Maybe you have seen the ads, or watched some of the TV programs. You may be very interested in learning about your own family tree. But where do you *really* start?

For me, genealogy is more than just a collection of names and dates. I went into the field because I want to know *who my ancestors were*. They may no longer be with us, but they are the reason I am here today. They were people, not just a bunch of names and dates listed in a dusty book or stored in a database. They had hopes, dreams, and needs, just as we all do. Through my research I am able to make connections, and watch personal stories unfold before me.

All kinds of people are interested in learning more about their roots. Do any of the following profiles seem familiar?

➤ **Sarah's grandmother always told her that the family came to North America on the *Mayflower,*** but no one ever seemed to believe the story. Curious, Sarah started to research her family history to see if her grandmother was right. Soon, she not only found one, but several *Mayflower* ancestors, and a fascinating family tree with roots across colonial New England. Thanksgiving now takes on a special meaning at her home. As she digs deeper into the family's history, the whole family loves learning about her discoveries.

➤ **John was adopted at birth and now wants to connect with his biological family.** Using what little information he knows about his origins, he has tried searching online and through paper records, but has not been able to find much. John has now turned to DNA testing with the hope that he can find a relative who will help him fill in his family tree and lead him to his birth parents.

➤ **Rose is of African-American heritage and wants to know more about the origins of her family.** Her grandparents did not talk much about growing up in Georgia, or about their extended families. Moreover, several records were destroyed in a house fire. Rose is certain that if she goes back far enough, she will find ancestors who were slaves. Nevertheless, she has a strong desire to know their stories.

➤ **David's father said the family's surname was changed at Ellis Island when their immigrant ancestor arrived in 1882.** After a visit to Ellis Island for a school trip, David discovered that the family legend was not supported by evidence in immigration records. Curious about why his great-grandfather, who was from Prussia, may have changed his name after arriving, David has begun to research his family history. He hopes one day he will be able to find records in Eastern Europe, where his family originated.

➤ **After Margaret's mother died, Margaret was cleaning out the attic.** She found a trunk full of letters, a family Bible, and old photographs. No one in the family recognizes the people in those photos, but Margaret noticed her mother's maiden name on the backs of several of the pictures. She has begun to reach out to cousins far and wide. One day she hopes to learn the identities of all of the people in the old photos, and where they came from.

Later, I will share more information about these cases. The names are not real, but the situations are based on real family research situations that can give you insights into your own genealogy quests.

What's in this guide

Genealogy has been around for hundreds of years in Europe. At first, it was a way for heralds to track noble families. At the end of the 19th Century, genealogy became a way for Americans to document their lineage—both Old World and Native American lines. In the 1970s, Alex Haley's *Roots* came to the small screen, energizing a new generation to seek out their family origins.

Genealogy is now booming. Thanks to an array of new tools and information sources, there has never been a better time to learn about your family's history. But the process can be daunting.

That's where this guide comes into play. This short guide will not only explain basic concepts and methods for family research, but it will also help you approach your research tasks in a smarter way that will save time and hopefully lead to better results. Topics include:

➤ The best approach to building a family tree and charting your research

➤ The most important records to look for

➤ Five things that can really trip up newbies (and tips for avoiding them)

➤ Dealing with "brick walls" in family research

➤ Approaching relatives for records, information, and family stories

➤ Research road trips, and what to bring in your portable genealogy kit

➤ The promise and perils of online research

➤ Getting started with genetic genealogy

➤ How to properly cite your findings

➤ Preserving family records and research for the next generation

We only have 30 minutes, so let's get started!

If you're interested in learning more about this title, or buying the ebook or paperback, visit the official website located at genealogy.in30minutes.com.

Notes

Notes

Notes

Made in the USA
San Bernardino, CA
12 March 2019